ISRAEL AND THE DIASPORA

by
BEN ZION DINUR

with an introduction by

YITZSHAK BAER

The Jewish Publication Society of America

PHILADELPHIA

1969-5279

The material for Books One and Two
was translated from the Hebrew
by Merton B. Dagut,
Lecturer in English Language
at the University College of Haifa.

Book Three originally appeared
in *The Jews, Their History, Culture and Religion,*
Third Edition, edited by Louis Finkelstein,
under the title,
"The Historical Foundations of the Rebirth of Israel,"
and is here republished with the permission of
Harper & Row Publishers, Inc.

CONTENTS

INTRODUCTION

BEN ZION DINUR (DINABURG)
The Jewish Historian

Ben Zion Dinur, dean of contemporary Jewish historians, reached his eighty-fifth year on the last day of Hannukah, 5728 (December 22, 1968). The first appearance in
a Western language of a selection from his writings re-
quires some words of introduction, so that a distant audi-
ence may become familiar with a great man whose many
books and articles have been published heretofore only in
Hebrew—with the exception of his earliest articles, which
he wrote in Yiddish and Russian. For a considerable time
now, Dinur, by virtue of his many unique abilities, has
held the first rank in the Jewish historiography of our generation. His work encompasses Jewish history from the
patriarchal era to contemporary times. Dinur is thoroughly
versed in the entire range of Hebrew literature, from the
earliest source material of Israel's faith and religion, the
books of the Bible, the Talmud, and commentaries, the
secular and religious poetry, the literature of Kabbalah and
Hasidism, through modern Hebrew literature and the
work of contemporary publicists. His critical historical
education and his political and pedogogical talents enabled him to assume an active role in the Zionist movement and in the establishment of the State of Israel, as
well as in her spiritual development. In addition to all the
above, Dinur is a gifted Hebrew writer, one who knows
how to write of what his eyes saw and of what occurred
in his surroundings and in his time.

His autobiography, which he has begun to write, is in
itself an important historical and literary document. Two

volumes have appeared to date: *Memories and Impressions from the Path of Life:* 1) *In the World That Set;* and 2) *In the Days of War and Revolution* (Bialik Institute, Jerusalem, 1958–1961).

Dinur was born and grew up in a Jewish township in the Ukraine, in a world whose entire spiritual content centered around talmudic and hasidic learning. He studied at the Tels Yeshiva and at the Liubavitch Yeshiva and qualified for rabbinic ordination. All that he learned in his youth remained fast in his heart and in his wonderful memory and served as a basis for his later historical research. Even during his days as a yeshiva student the Talmud began to change form in his eyes from a vessel of holiness to a basis of historical research. He turned toward the Jewish Enlightenment circles in Vilna, to the Socialist-Zionist movement, to the study of Jewish and general history. His political activity, from the time of the Kishinev pogrom (1903) and through the Bolshevik Revolution, and then his immigration to Eretz Yisrael, are described in detail in his memoirs. His journey to Berlin in 1911 was to become decisive for his scientific development, and his association there with Eugene Täubler, pupil of Theodore Mommsen, was a decisive one. Täubler himself was a great student of ancient history (he died in 1953). Under Täubler's tutelage and from his studies at the *Hochschule für die Wissenschaft des Judentums* and the Universities of Berlin and of Berne, Dinur learned to use a critical approach to the study of ancient Jewish history (the periods of the Bible, Second Commonwealth, and the Talmud) and of ancient Greece and Rome. As a fruit of his labors, in 1916 he presented to the noted Russian Rostovtzeff his dissertation *The Jewish Community in*

Palestine, the Roman Administration, and the Jewish Self-Government. This work, which was accepted by Rostovtzeff with acclaim, was lost during the time Dinur was making his preparations to immigrate to Eretz Yisrael. At at later date, gleaning from his memory and from some of his notes, Dinur managed to publish one of the chapters of his dissertation, entitled, "The Rescript of Diocletian to Judea in 293 and the Struggle Between the Nassi and the Sanhedrin in Eretz Yisrael." (Published in the memorial book of Asher Gulak and Samuel Klein, 1942.) This article is clear proof of Dinur's erudition in Talmud and Midrash, and in the legal and literary sources of Ancient Rome. The loss of his first important and comprehensive research was apparently one of the causes for the delay in Dinur's academic career. In 1919 Täubler invited him to return to Berlin as a research fellow in the Academy of Jewish Studies, which was then beginning its work.

Dinur immigrated to Eretz Yisrael in 1921 and worked in the Teachers' Seminary in Bet Hakerem from 1923–1948, first as a teacher and then as its noted director and as an educator of national importance. He considered the core of education to be the study of Bible and Jewish history.

He wrote and published essays, research articles, and books in early contemporary Jewish history.

Dinur has been since 1924 one of the contributing editors of the bibliographic quarterly *Kiryat-Sefer.* In 1926 there appeared the first volume of his *History of Israel in the Diaspora*—the first part of his life's work, about which we shall speak in detail later—and the first volume of *Zion—a Periodical issued by the Palestine Historical and Ethnographical Society.* In this periodical appeared the original research article by Dinur, "On Jewish History in Eretz Yisrael in the Days of the First Crusade," and the essay "The House of Prayer and Study for Jews on the Temple Mount" (1929)—a convincing essay that held the attention of the community last year when the Temple Mount became an actual reality within the domain of Jewish rule.

In the years 1932–1933 there appeared the two volumes of *Hibath Zion* (from its beginnings through Ahad Ha-Am), an interesting and informative work. In 1935, in the jubilee book dedicated to Rabbi David Yellin, Dinur published his excellent article "Rabbi Yehuda Halevi's Pilgrimage to Eretz Yisrael," an essay that sets the thought and poetry of the philosopher-poet for the first time in the context of the real world of his day.

Since 1936 Dinur served as lecturer (and since 1948 as professor) at the Hebrew University in Jerusalem. There was thus afforded him ample opportunity to influence the development of history courses and research projects in the university's curriculum.

Also in 1936 there appeared the first issue of *Zion—A Quarterly for Research in Jewish History, Issued by the Palestine Historical and Ethnographic Society*. This quarterly superceded the previous journal *Zion*, and continues to this day to fulfill its role in Jewish historical research. Dinur was and has remained the central dynamic initiator and creative force of this quarterly and of all that has since been undertaken under the aegis of the Society, whose name was changed in 1948 to The Israel Historical Society. It established The General Archives in Jewish History, which has now become a governmental institution. A considerable time ago, the Society began to publish the *Sefer Hayishuv*, giving expression to one of Dinur's fundamental concepts: Eretz Yisrael as the center and pivotal point of Jewish history. To this historical view Dinur devoted many articles and books: the Introduction to *Israel in the Diaspora*; *The Book of Zionism, Volume I: The Heralds of Zionism* (1939); and articles and speeches in which he presents the historical foundations of the State of Israel. Connected in an interesting way to this concept is the great essay "The Beginnings of Hasidism and Its Social and Messianic Elements." This essay first appeared in installments in the quarterly *Zion*, 1943–1945, and subsequently in a book titled *At Historical Crossroads*, Dinur, *Historical Writings*, Vol. I, (Bialik Institute, 1955). This essay constitutes a renewal of the author's youthful memories, and bears witness to his deep involvement in the ethical and hasidic literatures. Dinur describes in detail those social forces within Jewish society in the 18th century that were the forerunners of the Hasidic movement. Against the prevailing decadence of the community, Israel Ba'al Shem Tov rose up to redeem the people from its social and spiritual depression, as a prophet and teacher of a new messianic Torah, as a preacher for immigration to the Land of Israel for the sake of renewing the prophecy: "When every man shall experience a personal redemption—redemption of the soul which is in exile with the evil inclination—only then will there be general redemption."

There remains great objective value in the picture of Jewish society of that period as drawn by Dinur, though he did reveal in that study dormant qualities of his own self-image. In no other place did he speak with such emphasis of the religious relationship between the Land, the Jewish community, and the individual Jew. During the years of his service as Minister of Education and Culture for the State of Israel (1951–1955), he worked principally as a realistic national educator, and in the recent eventful year of national inspiration he refrained from raising his voice on controversial matters.

Since his years of study in the seminaries of Western Europe Dinur has remained involved in biblical research. Evidence of this interest are the first sections of *Israel in Her Land* and several articles: "The Story of the Conquest of Jerusalem in the Days of David and Its Historical Significance" (*Zion*, Vol. XI); "The Religious Image of the Cities of Refuge and their Ceremony of Offering Refuge" (*Eretz Yisrael*, 1954); "Psalm 139 and Its Historical Implications" (*Yitzhak F. Baer Jubilee Volume*, Jerusalem, 1960); "The Gideon Episode" (Dinur-Torczyner, *Studies in the Book of Judges*, 1966), and his profound study "The Image of Zion and Jerusalem in Israel's Historical Consciousness" (*Zion*, Vol. XVI).

In his old age Dinur turned his attention to the tasks which had occupied him during his early years in Russia. In 1960 the first volume of his monumental work, *The History of Israel, Original Sources and Documents, from the Beginnings of Israel to Contemporary Times*, began to appear in a new edition. Almost every year he now published a book of 500–700 pages! This is a gigantic undertaking by an aged scholar who is not at all healthy, who in the main does all his work by himself, and who has control over all his work by virtue of his amazing memory. Each volume includes—or is destined to include—four books. Their topics are: the position of the Jews in their land and in the lands of their dispersion; the changes wrought by the conditions of each era on the Jewish communities and on their centers in the East and the West; centers of Torah and culture; messianic fermentations; persecutions and conversions; and the last: "The World View of the Jew."

The fundamental principle of this superb work is to let the sources speak for themselves. The author explained his plan in the lecture (published in *Poel Hatzair*, 26 Adar II, February–March, 1965): "What Brought Me to My Approach in the Writing of Jewish History?" Clearly, problems arise, particularly with regard to outside sources. But as regards the Hebrew sources, every erstwhile critic has been awed by the abundance of the author's ideas and by the wisdom of his analysis. Some of his material seems to be that which is known to experts in the field, but—in addition to the documents and the many sections of manuscripts that were transcribed—the author knowledgeably and penetratingly coalesces diverse ideas into a unity, something no one else has been able to achieve in a single work, a unity that casts a new light upon both known and hitherto unknown historical phenomena. The reader of the work stands awed by the abundance of the author's ideas, by his penetrating wisdom and his acute analysis.

Let us wish our dear and revered friend long life and health, so that he may continue his work, and may he yet bring to light those many great works which are still within him!

Jerusalem   Yitzhak Baer
1st Day of Hannukah, 1968

BOOK
I

ISRAEL
IN
DIASPORA

I

I date the beginning of the era of "Israel in the Diaspora" from the Arab conquest of Palestine.

My reason for not choosing an earlier starting-point is that, until this date, Jewish history was, in the main, the history of the Jewish people living in its own land. This is so in spite of three facts of cardinal importance: (1) the antiquity of the Jewish Dispersion, the origins of which may be presumed to go back to before the destruction of the Northern Kingdom;[1] (2) the large number of Diaspora Jewish settlements and communities already existing in the time of the Roman and Byzantine empires (three hundred of them are known to us by name); and (3), the fact that, in this same period, the majority of the Jewish nation was living outside the borders of its own land.

In deciding on such a late starting-point for the Dispersion, the above facts notwithstanding, I have employed two criteria: first, the difference between the mere existence of scattered Jewish communities in foreign lands and the actual concept of "Israel in Diaspora"; and, secondly, the special historical character of "Israel in Diaspora."

The existence of scattered groups of a nation in foreign lands is not a phenomenon peculiar to the Jews. Throughout ancient history many peoples had settlements of their own kith and kin dotted about in other countries. Nor, indeed, was the phenomenon of "exile" (i.e., the deportation of a nation from its native soil) a fate especially reserved for the Jews alone. The Assyrians, as we know, followed a systematic policy of thus deporting whole nations for security reasons, a policy described by the Jewish sages as "mixing up the world." The unique

3

feature of "Israel in Diaspora," then, is not to be found in the expulsion of the Jews from their homeland to foreign countries, but in the continuation of collective Jewish life in the Dispersion and in spite of the Dispersion.

Accordingly, in the phenomenon of "Israel in Diaspora" (i.e., the existence of the Jews as a people without a country) two main factors must be distinguished: (1) the gradual disappearance of the specifically Jewish character of Palestine and the emergence of a different national majority in the country; (2) the survival of the Jewish nation and the preservation of its national character outside its own land, in periods when that land had ceased to be Jewish.

It is not, I think, necessary to go to any great length to prove that the real "Exile" (with regard to the *nation* as a collective historical body, and not with regard to its *individual members*) did not begin till the moment when Palestine ceased to be a Jewish country through being occupied and permanently settled by non-Jews. It is only from the time when the nation was deprived of the soil on which it had developed its own specifically national form of life that the problem of the individual Jew's preservation of their national character in the Dispersion became particularly acute. But when did this change occur, and how did it come about? This, in my opinion, is the most important question in the study of post-destruction Jewish history, just as the fact which the answer to this question seeks to explain is the decisive fact in the national life of the Jews after the loss of their national independence.

Jewish tradition and popular belief, it is true, do not make any distinction between the destruction of Jewish sovereignty in Palestine and the nation's loss of its own territory, but regard them as one and the same. From the historical standpoint, however, such a distinction must be made, since the two situations are not only separated in time, but are also different in their historical character.

It is true, of course, that they both resulted from historical processes which were the outward manifestation of a prolonged and bitter struggle, lasting for generations, waged by a nation now buoyed up by hope and now sunk in despair, now rebelling against the conqueror and now conforming to his will. Even the destruction of Jewish sovereignty in Palestine was not a single event, nor yet a series of events, but a long, fluctuating historical development, beginning with Pompey's conquest of the country and its partition by Gabinius, and only ending with the abolition of the Patriarchate in the reign of Theodosius II. This was a political and administrative process, in which the main factors were the Roman conquests in the Near East, the spread of Roman rule, and the consequent development of the Roman system of provincial government throughout the empire and particularly in the countries of the Near East. The territorial dispossession of the Jewish nation, on the other hand, was a social and colonizing process (though set, of course, in a certain political framework) in which the principal factors were, first, the continuous penetration of nomad desert tribes into Palestine and their amalgamation with the non-Jewish (Syro-Aramean) elements of the population; and, secondly, the domination of the country's agriculture by the new conquerors and the expropriation of Jewish lands for their benefit.

This was a long process. Its earliest beginnings go back

to the reign of Hadrian, when the Roman government, in pursuance of its aim of obliterating all record of the Jewish state (the name "Judah" was now changed to "Palestine"), started a systematic harassment of the Jews, while strengthening and increasing the numbers of the non-Jewish settlements; and it finally ended with the ruthless slaughter of the remaining Jewish population of the country by the warriors of the Crusades, "the vanguard of western civilization," who vented the stored-up Christian hatred of generations on "the enemies of God," and whose crusading fervor was as much the result of their hunger for land and their desire to conquer Palestine and rule it as of their religious faith.

However, the decisive event in this long struggle was the Arab conquest of Palestine, with the resulting expropriation of Jewish lands by the conquerors and the emergence of a new national majority in the country. This, therefore, is the right moment to choose as the starting-point of the era of "Israel in the Diaspora."

II

The first phase of the history of the Diaspora ends with the Crusades. Not only did this movement as such, together with its political and economic consequences, have a catastrophic effect on the life of the Jewish people and its status in all the lands of the Dispersion, but it also brought about profound changes in Palestine itself. Even after the predominantly Jewish character of Palestine had become a thing of the past, the country had still continued

6

to have a sizable Jewish population and the physical connection between the people and its land had remained unbroken. The Jews were at no time a nation without a country, but rather, even in the Exile, a nation which had been dispossessed of its soil by force and which had never ceased to protest against this act of political robbery and to demand the return of its stolen property. Throughout the long generations of the Dispersion every Jew firmly believed that "the Land is Israel's everlasting possession, which only they shall inherit and in which only they shall settle, and if perchance they are exiled from it they will return to it again, for it is theirs in perpetuity and no other nation's."[2]

This was not merely an ideological slogan, nor the messianic dream of unworldly visionaries, but a vividly felt and living attachment which found expression in deeds no less than in words. Every critical juncture in the history of Palestine from the Arab conquest down to our own times—starting with the civil war during the decline of the Umayyad dynasty (744–750) and ending with Mehmet Ali's conquest and his granting of concessions to foreign powers (1832–1842)—set off a wave of immigration amongst the Jewish masses to the Land of Israel.

However, despite this strong ideological attachment to Palestine, which in some measure found expression in Jewish customs and beliefs, the daily life of Diaspora Jewry was determined by entirely different factors. The Jews were obliged to come to terms with reality. They did not merely take up residence in other countries, but became firmly established in them, conforming to their way of life, taking root in their soil and adopting their culture, in accordance with the different conditions in each particular case. Nor were all these "passive" processes which took place automatically "through the force of circumstances." On the contrary, every such act of taking root in the countries of the Dispersion and of self-adaptation to their customs and cultures was achieved only after a hard struggle which had to be waged not only with the authorities and native populations of the countries in which the Jews had managed to obtain a foothold, but also against the inner Jewish feeling of "otherness" with regard to "foreign lands."

The success of this struggle was obviously bound to weaken the link between the nation and its own land. Evidence of this can be found in Jehudah Halevi's well-known admission, in his *Cuzari*, that the repetition by the Jews of his time of such expressions as "Bow down to His holy mountain," "Bow down to His footstool" and "Who restoreth His Presence to Zion" and the like are "mere twittering, since we do not think about what is said in these and other passages."[3]

This is a true reflection of one of the fundamental features of the spiritual life of Diaspora Judaism, even though it is also no doubt an expression of the poet's personal attitude to the Exile and the Redemption. Certainly, the Return to Zion and the anticipated Coming of the Messiah were not always the basic themes of medieval Jewish religious poetry. If there were times when Jews had to be called on to solemnly abjure messianic fervor, there were also times when the oath not to forget the messianic vision[4] was the one most needed.

The character of every single period of Jewish history in the Diaspora, and the various processes of transition from one to another, are determined by these two diametrically opposed tendencies: at the one extreme there

8

is stability and the effort to take permanent root in the lands of the Dispersion and to achieve the greatest possible degree of conformity to their ways of life; and, at the other, a feeling of insecurity and utter strangeness in these foreign lands and an eager expectation of imminent redemption. These two "poles" are connected with each other like the two highest points in the swing of a pendulum: the one must inevitably be followed by the other. Thus the shadow of crisis hangs over every period of stability in the lands of the Diaspora, since it is precisely the success of the Jews in establishing themselves in these countries and in adapting themselves to their ways of life that enlarges the area of friction and conflict with the native population. Hence, after every period of general "stability" there is a crisis of proportionately wide dimensions, and every period of maximum cultural conformity is followed by one of a growing sense of insecurity and strangeness, leading finally to a revival of the bond between the nation and its land, an outburst of messianic fervor, and a stream of immigration to Palestine, slow or rapid, small or large, according to the state of the country at the time. In other words, every crisis in the situation of Diaspora Jewry—from the Crusades, the persecutions sparked by the Black Death, and the expulsion from Spain, down to the pogroms of the eighties of the last century—set off a fresh wave of immigration to Palestine.[5]

The connection between the nation and its land can therefore serve us as a criterion for determining both the political condition of Palestine and the status of the Jews in the Diaspora. The strength of this bond always bears a direct relation to the former and is in inverse proportion to the latter, being most powerfully effective in a period when both these factors exert their pull simultaneously in

9

the same direction. The great messianic movements of the Middle Ages swept through the Jewish masses in times when a catastrophic change in the status of Diaspora Jewry coincided with the fateful permutations in Palestine.

III

The history of the Jews in the Diaspora may therefore be divided into periods of stability and periods of crisis. During the first broad period of stability (636–1096), large concentrations of Jews settled in most of the countries in which they were to be found in later times too, penetrated into all branches of economic life, from agriculture and ownership of land and property to posts in the administration, and also obtained a monopoly of certain economic functions (the handling of international trade and the management of the financial affairs of the new governments). It was in this period that the foundations were laid of that *modus vivendi* which enabled the Jewish communities of the Diaspora to survive in later periods of crisis: the non-Jewish majority accepted the existence in their midst of groups of permanent residents who nevertheless remained permanent foreigners and incorrigible and unrepentant "heretics"; while the Jewish minority adopted many of the customs and manners of the majority, and spoke, and even wrote, its language. The authorities' *de jure* recognition of the existence of these groups and of their own duty to protect them found outward expression in the "Jewish Charter," and in the establishment of autonomous Jewish institutions (the offices of

"Head of the Exile" and *Nasi,* the communal organizations, etc.) and the legal definition of their powers.

It is true that this whole intricate and ramified complex of Jewish rights and duties was the cumulative result of a long process and did not suddenly spring into being in this one period. But it was only now that it was accepted as one of the permanent and unquestioned bases of the general social order. The Jews had "become naturalized." Though they did not actually become part of the territorially based national groupings which, after generations of intermingling, now emerged in their more or less definitive forms, they were nevertheless firmly and closely linked both to their countries of residence and to the peoples in whose midst they lived.

It was in this period that the different territorial types of Jew came into being: the "Moghrabi" from North Africa, the "Sefardi" from Spain, the Jew from Christian lands, and from Greece, the French, the Italian, the "Ashkenazi" from Germany, and the resident in "the land of Canaan" (the Slavic countries). The Babylonian Jew of this period was also different in type from his forebears of the talmudic era. For the time being, it is true, there were no noticeable practical consequences of this fissiparous tendency in Judaism: on the contrary, the Jews owed the positions of special influence that they gained in economics (international trade), politics (international mediation) and culture (translations) to their national unity in dispersion resulting from the ties frequently existing between the Jews of different countries. But, for all that, there is no doubt that the origins of the divisions in Jewry which are felt in the following periods are to be found in the first period of stability in the Diaspora.

At this point several objections may be raised. First of

11

all, it may be argued that, while all the phenomena mentioned above are indications of the "stability" of the Jews in the various lands of the Diaspora and of the ways in which they struck roots in them, they apply only to this first phase and are not sufficient to substantiate the *general* division of the history of "Israel in Diaspora" into periods of stability and periods of crisis. Secondly, the true nature of historical events and happenings cannot be understood solely from their factual content, nor can they be placed in a certain general framework on the basis of this content alone: for this purpose they must first be interpreted in the light of a thorough study of their origins and causes. A third possible objection is that, if we trace the causes of all the phenomena listed above back to their source, we shall be led to conclude that practically all of them resulted from events which took place, in the main, outside the Jewish world and in connection with historical processes which were virtually confined to certain countries. In that case, is there not something oversimplified and artificially systematized about our attempt to make Jewish history in all the lands of the Diaspora conform to a single overall pattern which seemingly takes account only of the dates of the events, without attaching sufficient weight to the geographical factor? Would it not be more correct to adopt the method, first proposed by Dubnow, of drawing the dividing lines between the various phases of Jewish history in the Diaspora according to the shifts in the main centers of Jewish life? Must we not, indeed, concede that "in every period the Jewish people had one particular cultural center which, by the intensity of its inner life and the extent of its national and cultural autonomy, dominated and influenced all the others"?[6] Or was Graetz right in his contention that, although the history of the Jewish

Dispersion is the history of the whole nation and not merely that of its literature and scholars, "it is nevertheless essentially the history of its culture, which has been kept alive by the whole people"?[7] In which case, the correct conclusion would be that the distinctive character of the different phases of Jewish history in the Diaspora has been determined by changes in systems of religious thought and methods of expounding the Torah and Talmud, and by new trends in Hebrew literature, and that these are therefore the true criteria for fixing the chronological limits of each particular phase. Again, it may be questioned whether the fact that, in certain periods, there were messianic movements in various lands of the Diaspora and attempts at immigration to Palestine really tells us anything at all about the place occupied by the Land of Israel and its Jewish population in the general history of Diaspora Judaism. On the contrary, it may well be true that throughout the generations of the Exile, when the Jewish homeland was only a tiny geographical point on the three continents in which the Jews were scattered, the Diaspora remained cut off from Palestine and the *Yishuv* and received no influence of any real significance from them. Finally, is there perhaps some truth in the extreme contention that, with the exile of the Jews from their own land and their dispersion among the gentiles, the history of the Jewish nation came to an end, and that the subsequent vicissitudes of the various scattered Diaspora communities form part of the histories of the nations in whose midst they lived and are still living, of the countries in which they settled and are still residing, and of the constantly developing fabric of the social orders and political regimes into which the special Jewish way of life was interwoven?

IV

Our first task, therefore, before we can arrive at a proper understanding of Jewish history, is to clarify the following five fundamental points: (1) the unity of the nation during the period of its exile and dispersion; (2) the nature of this unity; (3) the nation's power of independent action in the Diaspora; (4) the reciprocal relations existing between the scattered Diaspora communities; and (5) the place occupied by the Land of Israel in the life of the exiled nation.

(1) The unity of the nation. *Were the Jews still really a single nation, even after they had been exiled from their land and dispersed over many countries, living amongst foreign peoples in a variety of different states? Can it be said that, even in these circumstances, the Jewish people still formed one organically united nation, the members of which were held together by permanent social bonds that drew their strength from a common life and destiny, and functioned in a social, national and—however tenuous— organizational framework, in spite of exile, dispersion, homelessness and oppression?*

(2) The nature of the nation's unity in exile. *Would it not be more correct to regard the unity of the nation in the Diaspora as purely religious? Was the "common life" —insofar as it existed at all—in fact any more than the common observance of the precepts of the Law and the common heritage of religious rituals and practices? And can the "common destiny" be regarded as in fact anything more than the similar plight of the Jews in various lands resulting from the form and development of the social*

and political systems in those lands, which were, so to speak, external "data" in no way dependent on the Jews themselves? Should we not, therefore, regard Saadiah Gaon's statement that "our nation is not a nation, except in its laws"[8] as an expression of the fundamental change that occurred in the Diaspora in the character of the nation's unity, which was now a unity restricted to the confines of "its laws"—its religious beliefs and doctrines and the rituals and practices connected with them—and ceased to be an all-embracing, organic unity nurtured by a "common life" and a "common destiny" of which the "laws" were only a part?

(3) The nation's power of independent action in the Diaspora. *Is it at all possible to regard Jewish history in the Diaspora as the* history of a nation? *Is it not rather the record of the vicissitudes of separate Jewish communities living in different historical frameworks? Have we any right to speak of the history of the nation in exile when it was, in fact, deprived of all "power of independent political action"? Should we not, therefore, consider it perfectly natural that the nation's power of independent action in exile was limited to the spiritual spheres of religious thought and practice, the only spheres of life in which the persecuted and homeless Jews were still their own masters? And does not this also lead us to the conclusion that Jewish history in the Diaspora is essentially the history of the religious element in Jewish life, in all its various manifestations and trends?*

(4) The reciprocal relations existing between the Jewish communities in the Diaspora. *The significance of the dispersion of the Jews does not lie only in their being*

15

scattered far and wide over many different countries. No less important than this is the fact that the separate settlements of Jews in these countries united to form whole communities, each one of which drew its strength from its own special common life and common destiny. To obtain a correct overall conception of Diaspora history we must, therefore, first form a clear picture of the part played by these different territorial groups of communities, and by the reciprocal relations between them, in determining the general character of the nation in exile and dispersion.

(5) The place of the Land of Israel in the life of the exiled nation. *The basic phenomenon of the period of the Diaspora is, without any doubt, the fact that the Jews were exiles from their own land, dispersed amongst the nations and living on foreign soil. Hence, in order to obtain a proper historical understanding of the Diaspora it is essential first to clarify the actual importance of this basic phenomenon as a* formative factor *in Jewish life. The best indications of this are to be found in the attitude of the Jews in the Dispersion to the Land of Israel and its Jewish population, and in the connection that existed between this attitude and their feeling of strangeness and home-lessness among the Gentiles.*

V

As a matter of fact, nearly every Jewish historian of recent generations has not merely tried to answer these questions, but has also done his best to formulate that answer, though not always in absolutely clear terms, as a rule of universal application. Indeed, the general development of modern Jewish historiography is largely reflected in the different approaches adopted by the historians to these questions and in the different types of answer sought to them.

The first of the Jewish historians of the nineteenth century, Isaac Mordecai Jost (1793–1860), divided the history of the Diaspora into that of Western and Eastern Jewry, and tried in his work to describe the historical vicissitudes of each of these groups separately.[9] According to Jost, the difference between the history of Eastern and Western Jewry is that, in the East, the main role is played by the Jewish community as a whole, whereas in the West it is the individual Jew who is of most importance. In the populous Jewish communities of the East, which were mainly concentrated in certain districts and regions, the sense of suffering and oppression was common to all, with the result that "the Jews were capable of taking concerted action, like the Armenians, the Syrians and the other peoples of these states," whereas in the West there was no Jewish public, but only Jewish individuals. "Jewish emigration to distant lands" (i.e. to western Europe), remarks Jost, "is the result of individual necessity. . . . It was not of their own inclination that the Jews in foreign lands became a separate, self-contained entity. . . . In the absence of any other uniting factor, they came together only for prayer; apart from the synagogue, there were no mutual bonds between them."[10] Indeed, the very survival of the Jews as a separate nation was due only to external conditions, and not to internal factors: it was brought about by the rejection of the Jews by the outside world, and not by any inner unifying forces. The sense of national unity binding together the Jews in the various lands of their dispersion resulted merely from the refusal of the gentiles to accept them into their own societies, or even to let them regard the countries in which they resided as their "fatherlands." But for this fact, the Jews of France and Italy would be no closer to each other than the Catholics of those countries. "The Jews remained a separate, self-contained entity, because others treated them as such."[11] The basis of Jost's division of the Jewish Diaspora into two halves is thus not only territorial, but also qualitative. In the countries of the East it is the history of a nation which, though conquered and enslaved, nevertheless actively struggles to determine its own fate; whereas in the West it is merely the record of the vicissitudes of a scattered and for the most part persecuted, despised and isolated religious community, which is the passive victim of events instead of the active initiator of them.

Jost's answers to our five questions, which are contained in this explicitly stated general historical conception of Diaspora Judaism, are still more clearly evident in his whole historiographical method—in the structure of his work, in the aspects of historical reality that mainly interest him, and in his evaluations of periods, trends and personalities. He does not appear to cast the slightest doubt on the reality of the unity of the Jewish people even in the Diaspora, although he regards this unity as forced on it from outside. Indeed, he even holds that "Judaism"—by which he means "the spiritual development of the nation after the destruction of its political life—"succeeded in welding the Jews together in an inner unity which was much stronger than in the days of their independence." Yet in the titles of his books Jost uses the term "Israelite" instead of "Jew": *The History of the Israelites from the Time of the Maccabees to the Present Day, A General History of the Israelite People,* and *The Modern History of the Israelites.* Only in his last work, which was deliberately restricted to a historical account of Jewish religious belief, is the more limited nature of the subject matter indicated by the wording of the title: *A History of Judaism and Its Sects.* Jost himself tried—without success—to find some plausible justification for his use of the term "Israelite" in reference to periods when there were no more "Israelites," but only "Jews." It can be shown from his own words that the real reason for his use of this term is to be found in the historical circumstances *of his own time,* and has no connection at all with his historical conception of the nation's unity. A clear indication of this is the fact that even the history of the Jews in their own Land during the period between the destruction of the Temple by Titus and the final capture of Betar (including the revolt of Bar Kokhba) are, for Jost, simply episodes in "the history of the Jews in the Roman empire," to which belong also the *Sanhedrin* at Jabne and the *Yeshivah* at Tiberias, the office of *Nasi* and its development, and also the compilation of the Mishnah and the Jerusalem Talmud. It is interesting and noteworthy that the only one of twenty-eight volumes of his great work in which Jost deals with features of Jewish life in the Diaspora common to all the scattered communities is the twenty-sixth. This volume contains "an account of the non-Rabbinical sects of Jews and other dissident Jewish communities, some of them in the Turkish empire and some of them in Christian lands or under pagan rule in Asia and Africa." "The dissident Jewish communities" in all the lands of the Diaspora are thus, for

19

Jost, a separate historical entity, whereas the compilation of the Babylonian Talmud, the work which united the whole of Jewry, belongs entirely and solely to the history of Babylonian Jewry.

It was only in his last book, A *History of Judaism and Its Sects*, that Jost found himself able to regard Judaism as a single unity. Here he marked off the various periods of its history according to the different stages of its inner development (from Ezra to the end of the compilation of the Talmud—the period of the Oral Law; and from the end of the Talmud to our own times—the writing down of the Oral Law). But in his account of this historical reality he places the main emphasis on the formation, character and influence of the institutions, regulations and laws of Judaism, regarding them as organic phenomena of the religion which are dependent only on its inner development.

Jost's answer to our five questions are thus clearly implied in his whole historiographical method as it appears in all his works:[12]

_(1)_ *The political unity of the Jewish nation in exile and dispersion was at best only partial; such unity as did exist was forced upon the nation by external pressures that obliged the Jews, for a time, to maintain specifically national Jewish institutions which subsequently, in the natural course of events, gradually disappeared.*

(2) *In contrast to the above, there was a geuine* religious unity, *forged partly by inner developments amongst the Jews themselves during their life in exile as an oppressed minority. Hence, Jewish history is, first and foremost, the history of the Jewish religion at every period and in every place.*[13]

20

(3) *The history of Diaspora Judaism is, according to Jost, primarily the record of the treatment of the Jews by other nations and states, and is thus inseparable from the histories of the countries in which the Jews resided and of the nations and states in whose midst and under the protection of whose laws they lived.*

(4) *The reciprocal relations existing between the Jewish communities in the various lands of the Diaspora are not a factor of any historical importance. They are of no particular interest to the historian, who need not record them or dwell on them at all.*

(5) *The role of the Land of Israel in the period of the Diaspora cannot be regarded as of any special significance, according to Jost. First, Palestine was part of the Roman and Byzantine empires; then, with the sweeping and rapid advance of the Moslems, it became part of their empire and the Jews of Palestine also came under their rule. From then onward the history of the Jews in Palestine belongs to the general history of the Jews in Islamic lands.*

The principal defect in Jost's historical standpoint is its lack of organic unity. His virtual denial of the existence of the one living and unifying factor—the nation—in the entire chain of events reduces his account to a mechanical combination and arrangement of separate events and incidents devoid of any inner, organic significance. It must be admitted, however, that Jost's views form a consistent whole and reflect the historical outlook of a generation. That is why expressions of this particular standpoint are so numerous in the whole field of Jewish historical research in that generation, and also why Jost's influence on Jewish historiography was more lasting and considerable than is commonly thought.[14]

VI

Graetz's answers to our five questions are not wholly satisfactory either. True, his method of writing Jewish history is very different from Jost's, being infused with a vividness and enthusiasm that brings the remote past to life for the reader by transporting him into it in his imagination. Nor is this achievement to be attributed solely to the historian's literary and scholarly gifts—the special emotional quality of his style which arouses the reader's active sympathy and lively admiration, and his command of the great wealth of fact and detail brought to light with the progress of scientific research. A still more important element in the vitality of Graetz's account is his grand conception of the whole Jewish nation, and not just individual Jews or even separate communities, as the formative factor in the history of the Diaspora. His historical approach is based on the unity in dispersion of the Jewish nation, a unity which he repeatedly emphasizes and the nature and quality of which he explains again and again.

This conception first appears in the introduction to the fourth part of his work where Gratez describes the Jewish communities as "all standing in one wide circle around the ruins of the Temple, which had lost none of its sanctity even though reduced to ashes. . . ."[15] In the introduction to the fifth part he develops this theme and stresses that, even in the post-talmudic period, Judaism continued

22

to preserve its national character and that its history was in no sense merely the history of a creed or a religious sect. "The subject-matter of Jewish history is not only the course followed by the development of Jewish religious law, but also the fate of a national tribe."[16] This national tribe, "it is true, had no soil, no homeland, no clearly demarcated geographical borders, and no political organization; but it made good the lack of these physical conditions of nationhood by its spiritual powers."[17] Again: "Though dispersed throughout the civilized world and permanently settled in their countries of residence, the members of the Jewish tribe never ceased to feel that they were a single national entity bound together by a common religious awareness, common historical memories, and common customs and hopes."[18] Moreover, this unity was not, in Graetz's opinion, merely a matter of sentiment, but was also embodied in concrete outward forms. "Although the scepter was taken from Judah, the lawgiver has never departed from his sons."[19] It is these lawgivers, the true creators of the religio-national ethos, that have in every generation been the heart of the nation and have acted as the bond uniting the scattered communities of the Diaspora into a single entity. It is quite wrong to suppose that, in the history of Jews in Diaspora, there has been no "centripetal movement." On the contrary, it is a definite and striking fact that several centers, from which Jewish life radiated in a wide circle, were created in the course of Diaspora history: "Jewish Babylon," the seat of the *Geonim*; the prolific and dynamic "new center of gravity" in Spain; and the associated centers of Torah and *Haskalah* in southern and northern France.[20]

However, it was not by these geographical shifts in the

religious center of Jewry that Graetz actually divided up the history of the Diaspora, but according to the different methods of the study of the Torah. In distinguishing the various chronological phases of this long period, he took as his criterion the dominant spiritual and religious trends in Jewish literature in each of the talmudic, the rabbinic-philosophical, and the rabbinical periods. "Jewish literature," remarks Graetz, "is the kernel of Jewish history, and the nation's sufferings and misfortunes its bitter skin. It is on the thread of this literature that we must therefore string our chronological account of all the facts and events, since it alone provides us with the pragmatic connection between them."[21]

Graetz also differs from Jost in his formulation of the relationship between Jewish and general history in the Diaspora period. "The Jews in the Dispersion," he writes, "shared in the great events of world history, were involved in the suffering caused by them, and were also, to a certain extent, active participants in them. Every violent upheaval of general historical import had repercussions deep inside Judaism too. . . . Jewish history during these seventeen centuries was thus universal history in miniature, just as the Jewish people had itself become universal: since it was nowhere in its own home, its home was everywhere."[22]

These ideas—the unity of the nation and the interconnection of its component parts, the spiritual nature of this relationship, and the active participation of the Jews in world history—were, so to speak, the cornerstones of Graetz's philosophy of Jewish history. At the same time, it must be stated that the historiographical structure of Gratez's works shows that he did not keep strictly within his own ideological framework. In his general approach he

24

does, it is true, distinguish periods by their spiritual character (the conclusion of the Talmud, the heyday of Jewish culture in Spain, and the *Haskalah,* the beginning of the "Mendelssohnian" period); but he also employs another, quite different, criterion—the fate of the large Jewish communities (the expulsion from Spain and Portugal, the permanent settlement of the Marranos in Holland).[23]

In this connection, it is interesting to note the division of Jewish history adopted by Graetz in his last book, a three-volume popular edition of his work. In the second and third of these volumes, which deal with the Dispersion, the author divides Jewish history from the Destruction of the Temple down to the revolution of 1848 and its aftermath into six periods: the transitional phase (from the Destruction to the coming of Islam), the period of the *Geonim,* the supremacy of Spanish Jewry, the Marrano interlude, the rise of humanism and the Reformation, and the period of national revival (the *Haskalah* and Jewish emancipation). What is interesting about this division is, on the one hand, the absence of any *spiritual and religious criterion* in the distinction of the various periods (the talmudic period has here become a "transitional phase," and "the heyday of Jewish culture in Spain" now appears simply as "the supremacy of Spanish Jewry"), and, on the other hand, the introduction of a new reference point from non-Jewish history (the rise of humanism and the Reformation).

Although Graetz was neither consistent nor systematic in the conclusions that he drew from his own general conception of Jewish history, his work as a whole provides a more or less clear answer to our five preliminary questions about Israel in the Diaspora:

(1)   The unity of the Jewish nation, even in dispersion, is the cornerstone of Graetz's whole historiographical method. In his account of every period, he gives a comprehensive historical survey of all the Jewish communities at that particular time.

(2)   This national unity is essentially spiritual (a common religious awareness, common historical memories and future hopes, etc.), and therefore the history of the nation is principally the record of the various manifestations of its spirit: its poetry and philosophy, its customs and manners.[24]

(3)   The history of the various Jewish communities is closely bound up not only with the histories of the lands in which they happen to be living, but also with world events, that is, with the periodic epoch-making changes that occurred simultaneously in all countries. The history of Diaspora Judaism is, moreover, not only the record of the treatment accorded to the Jews by other nations: the Jews are not only passively influenced by their surroundings, but also exert an active influence on them.[25]

(4)   The various Diaspora communities are parts of a single nation whose spiritual unity manifests itself in the reciprocal relations existing between them, and in the influence exerted by this or that community on the nation as a whole.

(5)   The Land of Israel has ceased to be a real factor in Jewish history. The whole of Jewish history from the Roman conquest to the coming of Islam, (including the Bar Kokhba revolt, Jabne, the Babylonian exilarchate, and the Mishnah down to the abolition of the exilarchate) is assigned by Graetz to the "transitional phase" between

26

statehood and exile; and Jewish history in Palestine in the period of the ascendancy of Safed is treated by him merely as part of the history of the Jews in Turkey. Insofar as Palestine had any significant influence on Jewish life it was only as part of the nation's "spiritual inheritance," as one of the elements of its spiritual unity.[26]

VII

However, when it came to applying this general formula to the detailed interpretation of the historical processes which constitute the chequered life history of Diaspora Jewry, Graetz did not go beyond the theoretical acknowledgment of the nation's spiritual unity, while in practice continuing to adhere to his earlier (1846) view of Jewish history in the Diaspora as a development conditioned by the organization of talmudic schools and the changes in their methods of study. He thus failed to advance beyond the opinions of Jost and his contemporaries. For what else is Graetz's well known characterization of the duality in the historical contents of Diaspora Judaism ("studying and wanderings, thinking and suffering, learning and being persecuted") but a virtual acceptance of Jost's historical standpoint? "The outward history of this period," writes Graetz, "is the record of the nation's sufferings and miseries, while the inner history is the record of its spirit." This is surely tantamount to saying that the outward history of Jewry in the Diaspora is the record of its treatment by other nations, while its inner history is "the course taken by the development of Jewish religious law."

It is a truism that the history of a dispersed people must

27

be closely bound up with that of the nations in whose midst it lives and of the countries in which it has made its home. But what is in question here is not the undisputed fact of this influence, which is one of the best known and most readily intelligible of historical phenomena, but its actual character and its importance in deciding the fate and status of the various scattered Jewish communities. This is just the point on which Graetz's treatment is not sufficiently clear or reasoned. Even his acknowledgment of the nation's unity remained, as we have noted, a theoretical abstraction: it never developed into a higher awareness of the nation as a living and, sometimes more sometimes less, self-sustaining entity; nor was the historian prompted by it to try to discover the different manifestations and expressions of this constantly varying unity in all the communities of the Diaspora. The "Jewish tribe" and the "Jewish law"[27] were never merged in Graetz's historical outlook into a single organic whole. Try as he may to give us a complete and comprehensive picture, in chronological sequence, of the events in the life of the nation throughout the Diaspora, generation by generation, all that he actually succeeds in producing is a literary combination of various separate details, arbitrarily brought together without any explanation or proof of their organic connection with each other or of their joint relation to their time. It is noteworthy that it is precisely in those features of Diaspora history in which the unity of the dispersed nation was most fully and completely displayed (the religious trends which affected all communities and classes, the messianic and mystic movements, etc.,) that Graetz failed as a historian, through his inability to hear the steady heartbeat of the nation's life under its changing outward guises. In this respect Geiger was, I think, undeniably right in maintaining that, in reading Graetz's book, we have no sense of historical development or historical motivation, nor are we made aware that there was an inner causality governing the emergence of the political and religious movements in which the deepest aspirations of a community bound together in a certain degree of spiritual unity found expression. Though we cannot accept Geiger's theological view of the nature of this inner causality (i.e., that there is some final point, some ultimate goal to which events, are directed and which the historian must therefore start from as his basic premise), there is no doubt that such a law of cause and effect is at work in history and that, without recognition of this, no adequate reconstruction of historical events in possible.[28]

VIII

The whole development of Jewish historiography from the time of Graetz onward has, in fact, been characterized by the endeavor to write a history of the events based on this "inner causality." It must be admitted, however, that the nature of the inner causality discerned by the different historians has depended on the spiritual character of their particular period; nor has it always been truly "inner"— that is, based on the common substratum underlying all the historical phenomena and facts. All too often historical consistency is achieved by the unwitting disregard of facts which could not be squared with dogmatic theories.[29] The most interesting and influential representative of the "inner causality" school of thought in Jewish history is Abraham Geiger (1810–1874).

Geiger's views were closely bound up with the problems of his own generation—the generation of Reform Judaism and of the struggle for Jewish emancipation and the full entrance of Jews into European society and its culture. In his constant desire to provide "a historical basis" for his solutions to these problems, Geiger tried to find the "historical roots" of the trend of developments in his own day, which he considered eminently desirable and thoroughly justified. Hence, Geiger's historical viewpoint should be regarded as a chapter in the history of modern Jewish political and social theorizing, since indeed the aims, trends and methods of historiography form an organic part of the general history of society's ideological thought. Geiger's opinions deserve special attention for two further reasons: first, because he injected his own special historical conception into all his scientific work and, in his original studies of all periods of Jewish history, also tried to lay down the framework of a thorough-going historiographical method in accordance with his own principles; and, secondly, because of his very great influence, even on those Jewish circles that were far removed from him both in outlook and in time.

In his earliest works Geiger already stressed that Jewish history since the destruction of the Temple was merely one long series of misfortunes and torments in which "there is no life-breath of history" but only "a putrid stench as from a field of corpses,"[30] and in which there is no place at all for any "rational principle of development." Post-exilic Jewish history is in fact only the history of Hebrew literature, or rather of that particular branch of it which reflects the spiritual and ideological development of Judaism—its belief and thought and its laws and customs. The task of "Jewish history" is to record, scientifically, the true development of biblical and talmudic Judaism which has now been replaced by the new ideas of modern times.[31]

The clearest exposition of this conception is found in his "General Introduction to the Science of Judaism" (*Allgemeine Einleitung in die Wissenschaft des Judenthums*). There he explicitly states his view that history, as an organic part of the Science of Judaism, can obviously be only the history of the nation's spirit, in which the record of external circumstances is of value only as providing the substratum of physical conditions that helped or hindered the nation's spiritual progress.[32] "It is part of the essential nature of the Jews that their history is mainly spiritual." Only in this respect have the Jews "served as a model to the world," whereas their political regime or social structures have not had any significant influence.

In accordance with this philosophy, Geiger divided Jewish history into the following four phases: revelation, tradition, rigid legalism, and critical approach. The first of these lasted from the earliest beginnings of the nation down to the closing of the Biblical canon; the second from the closing of the Biblical canon down to the final recension of the Talmud; the third from the final recension of the Babylonian Talmud to the middle of the eighteenth century; and the fourth from then to the present day.[33]

We see, then, that Geiger's conception of Jewish history provides clear and almost explicit answers to our five preliminary questions concerning the nature of Diaspora Judaism:

(1) *The nation continued to exist as a unity, and this unity is to be regarded as the subject of Jewish history.*

(2) *This unity is purely spiritual and religious, and Jewish history is, in fact, concerned only with the spiritual and religious spheres of Jewish life.*

(3) *Judaism was capable of independent action only in the spiritual sphere. In this sphere it continued to be an active and influential force at all times and in all periods.*

(4) *The relations between the various Jewish communities are also of historical importance to the extent that they make themselves felt in the spiritual sphere—in terms of reciprocal influence on religious belief and thought, religious laws and customs.*

(5) *The Land of Israel plays no part at all in post-exilic Jewish history.* Even though Geiger was of the opinion that the destruction of the Temple and the Exile "released" Judaism from the trammels of its territorial limits, he did not specify these events as a dividing line between two qualitatively different epochs of Jewish history. Admittedly, in his lectures on "Judaism and its History" (Das Judenthum und seine Geschichte) *the destruction of the Temple and of the Jewish state form the beginning of a period; but only because the "Exile" and the "wanderings among the nations" are an imperative part of the historical mission of Judaism, and not because they represent a turning point in the nation's destiny.* It was decreed that "the Jewish people" should wander about the world, taking with it the special form of life that it had created for itself. Judaism was commanded by Providence to "go out into the whole world, while preserving

32

in yourself the power which strengthens and purifies you and which will win over to you the whole of mankind."[34] In other words, exile and dispersion were also a stage in the inner development of Judaism.

However, when Geiger's doctrine of a Jewish mission is stripped of the theology and pathos with which he invested it, his views are found to be essentially the same as Jost's and likewise owe their self-consistency to the deliberate disregard of the historical fate of the Jews, which is treated by both these historians as a kind of external appendage to the true inner content of Jewish history.

IX

The first historian to suggest a new and, in many respects, fundamentally different approach to the history of the Diaspora was Simon Dubnow. In his first monograph "What Is Jewish History?"[35] Dubnow's standpoint is still, to all intents and purposes, that of Graetz. For Dubnow too "the history of Diaspora Judaism is merely an account of the triumphs of its spirit over the torments of its flesh." For him too the sole source of the nation's unity is its religious awareness, which took the place both of the no longer existent political bond and of the greatly weakened ethnical instinct.[36] However, Dubnow's application of the term "spirit" is far wider and more comprehensive than Graetz's. He stresses several times that the history of Diaspora Judaism is "a series of pictures of social customs, a long account of facts from the spiritual, ethical, religious and communal spheres"; that "if the true kernel of history is the inner life and social and spiritual development of the nation, while wars and politics are merely its outer shell, then the history of the Jews in the Diaspora is all kernel without shell." The Jewish nation in the Diaspora is thus united not only by the strength of its religious traditions and by its ability to endure all manner of misfortunes, but also by its unique capacity of "continuing to live as a nation in conditions under which no other people could survive."[37] Dubnow accordingly accepted, by and large, Graetz's chronological divisions of the whole period of the Diaspora, but at the same time he added a geographical criterion to Graetz's spiritual yardstick. The geonic age (500–980 C.E.) is thus equated by Dubnow with the ascendancy of Oriental Jewry; the rabbinic philosophic age (980–1492) with the hegemony of Spanish Jewry; and the mystical age (1492–1789) with the supremacy of German and Polish Jewry.[38]

On the question of the relation of Jewish to world history Dubnow also, in all essentials, merely explains and slightly expands Graetz's views. "The fate of this wandering people," writes Dubnow, "which is dispersed throughout the civilized world, is an integral part of the fate of the most influential nations and empires and of the various trends of general human thought. This organic connection is of a twofold nature: in periods of intellectual obscurantism and religious fanaticism the Jews are 'physically affected' by the nations in whose midst they live (persecutions and ruinous tolls, the Inquisition, etc.); and, conversely, in times of humanitarian enlightenment, the Jews draw closer to those same nations and are now influenced by them culturally and intellectually. At the same time, Jewry for its part exercises a continuous influence on the other nations, both by its intellectual creativeness (its philosophy and literature) and also by the very fact of its spiritual strength and vitality, by its whole historical character."[39] The Jews are thus not merely the passive recipients of outside influence, but also themselves exert an influence on others—but not "actively." Their influence is a *fact* and not a *factor*: it results from the mere passive existence of certain phenomena in Jewish life, and not from any concerted outward action on the part of the Jews, or from their joint participation in the lives of the gentile communities in whose midst they live.

Subsequently, however, Dubnow himself abandoned many of these early views.[40] "In studying Jewish history," he writes, "we have to solve the problem of how the Jewish people has created its history—first politically in the time when it had its own independent kingdom; and then socially, spiritually and culturally, when the political state was replaced by the autonomous Jewish community and the national and cultural ties of world Jewry. The two basic motive forces of Jewish history in the Diaspora are the autonomy of the separate communities, on the one hand, and the common national bond uniting the Jews of different countries, on the other."[41]

In accordance with this later formulation of his views, Dubnow advocated a new division of Diaspora history, this time not by literary epochs, but according to "the shift of the centers of Jewish hegemony." "In every period, the dispersed Jewish people had one particular cultural center which dominated and influenced all the others." The differences between the centers and their respective degrees of influence depended, in Dubnow's opinion, "on the intensity of their inner Jewish life and the extent of their national autonomy." By this criterion Dubnow distinguished four main centers in the history of the Diaspora: Palestine, in the period of the patriarchate; Babylon, in the period of the exilarchs; Spain "in the time of the cultural renaissance"; and finally, "the fourth great hegemony," that of Polish Jewry, which, in the sixteenth-eighteenth centuries, enjoyed a large measure of autonomy and had a model communal oganization, with local and central committees, until it eventually ceded its supremacy, in modern times, to Russian Jewry.[42]

Dubnow's historical views are most clearly evident in the historiographical layout of his great work *A World History of the Jewish People (Weltgeschichte des Jüdischen Volkes)*. The contents of the eight volumes of this book—which traces Jewish history from the overthrow of Judah down to the First World War—are divided into two main epochs: the Oriental, from the Roman conquest down to the decline of the Eastern centers of Jewish life; and the European, comprising the Middle Ages and modern times down to the present day. Within this general framework, the chronological division is by centers of Jewish life. The first section of the book, which deals with the thousand years and more from "the Destruction of the Second Temple to the decline of the Eastern centers," consists of three volumes covering three periods, each marked off from the others by the supremacy of the community whose influence on Judaism was decisive at the particular time: (1) the hegemony of Palestine, during the rule of pagan Rome; (2) the hegemony of Palestine and Babylonia, under the sway of Christian Rome, Byzantium and Persia; and (3) the hegemony of Babylonia, from the time of the Caliphate down to the decline of the Eastern centers. The second section, dealing with "the history of the Jewish people from the beginning of the European diaspora down to the end of the Crusades," is also divided into three volumes covering three periods: (1) "Jewish settlement in Europe till the Arab conquest of Spain"; (2) "the internal organization of European Jewry till the Crusades"; and (3) "the period of the Crusades." In actual fact, a considerable part of the matter dealt with in this section also belongs to the period of the hegemony of the Eastern centers. Next comes Jewish history in "the latter part of the Middle Ages" which comprises two periods: (1) "the Franco-Spanish hegemony"; and (2) "the Spanish-German hegemony." The history of modern times is similarly divided by Dubnow into two periods: (1) the expulsion from Spain and the German hegemony; and (2) the Polish-German hegemony. And the most recent phase of Jewish history is divided into four periods: (1) the first Emancipation; (2) the first Reaction; (3) the second Emancipation; and (4) the second Reaction.

Dubnow's historical views and the general historiographical structure of his first works thus provide clear answers, some explicit and others implied, to our five preliminary questions:

(1) The unity of the nation remained a unity in the full sense of the word, even when the nation was dispersed and oppressed.

(2) The unity of the nation in the Diaspora was, in fact, of a spiritual nature. The concept of "spirit," however, is not to be narrowly restricted only to the religious

sphere, but is to be extended to all fields of social life, except the political and military.

(3) Even as a dispersed and oppressed minority the Jews continued to create their own history. The scope of their historical activity, however, was reduced to the struggle for their physical survival and for the preservation of their spiritual independence.

(4) The existence of relations between the different Jewish communities is a historical fact. In every period there was one dominant community which constituted the focal point, as it were, of Jewish life.

(5) The Land of Israel was an important factor in Jewish life only during the period of the "Eastern centers." Since that time it has had no special influence and cannot therefore be regarded as a permanent factor in the history of Diaspora Judaism.

X

Dubnow's view gained acceptance, broadly speaking, amongst the Jewish intelligentsia and even, to a certain extent, amongst the mass of the Jewish population, without at the time being adequately elucidated by a thorough critical study. But some such elucidation is certainly necessary, since some of Dubnow's assumptions not only need to be proved, but are, I think, in several respects fundamentally unsound.

It is true that the organization of Jewish life in the Dispersion was based on the autonomous community. It is also true that these communities are to be regarded as the historically active centers in which the "motive forces" of Jewish history manifested themselves, and that their development is to be depicted as resulting from the functioning of those forces. But to identify the communities with the "motive forces" which produced them is to make the result into the cause. Still less is there any warrant for regarding "the cultural and national ties uniting world Jewry" as a "historical motive force," since the very existence of such ties, in some specific organized form and not just as a vague emotional awareness, itself stands in need of proof.

It is certainly true that the degree of reciprocal influence existing between the different Diaspora communities varied greatly and that it is the task of the historian of the Diaspora to single out for special mention just those communities which, by their intensely active inner life, exercised a dominating influence on all the others. But to determine "the centers of hegemony" by the criterion of their spiritual influence is putting the cart before the horse. The degree of influence exercised by this or that Jewish community in its own time cannot be judged by its effect on later generations. If, for example, we say that Spanish Jewry dominated the other communities of the Diaspora (in France, Germany, Italy, Africa and the Oriental countries), we must prove that its special influence was stronger and more lasting than that of other centers at that particular time. To postulate the existence of such an influence without a proper preliminary examination of the facts is tantamount to taking an unknown and unproven factor as the basis of the chronological division of the history of the Diaspora. For, in the present state of historical research,

Dubnow's dogmatic assertion that "in every period there was one main center" is in fact no more than an unproven assumption. All the centers listed by Dubnow were not the only main centers in the periods in question. Palestine continued to exercise a powerful influence over all the Diaspora communities — including even Babylonia — throughout the geonic period (which, in Dubnow's scheme, was the heyday of the "Babylonian center") and right on down to the Crusades; and during the same period Italian Jewry had a considerable influence on the Occidental communities. Again, the hegemony of Dubnow's third center, the Spanish one, coincided with the great days of the Franco-German center which, on Dubnow's own admission, "wedges itself into this period and claims a position of spiritual supremacy entirely independent of the Spanish hegemony."[43] Similarly, the rise of Polish Jewry occurred at the same time as the resurgence of Palestinian Jewry which had such special consequences (the Safed *Cabbalah* and the messianic movements); and it was also in this period that the Jewries of Italy and Holland were distinguished by a particularly intense inner life (the beginning of the *Haskalah* and the movement for emancipation), the influence of which was felt throughout the Diaspora. Conversely, the influence of Russian Jewry (which, according to Dubnow, took over the hegemony of the Diaspora from the Polish community) did not really begin until the second half of the nineteenth century.

Furthermore, this whole system of chronological division by "the shifts in the centers of influence" is much more in keeping with Graetz's historical conception, in which each of these centers represents a different trend in the development of the study of the Law, than with Dubnow's view, according to which the leading role in Jewish history in the Diaspoa is played by the "national unit," a political body like all other peoples, but one that continues its national life in conditions entirely different from those of other peoples. Such a view would logically oblige us to look for the centers of the nation not in those countries in which the fixed patterns of its special national way of life took shape, but rather in those lands in which there was the highest concentration of the "motive forces" of Jewish history, that is, in which the joint will of the nation and its power of independent action manifested themselves (one of the characteristic phenomena of the Diaspora being that these two factors are not always found together).

But this raises the question of how far it is possible to attribute a joint will and a power of concerted action to the scattered portions of a nation which were taking root in other countries and becoming integrated into other sovereign national groupings. In other words, we are back to the question about the relation of Diaspora history to general history. And this question can most certainly not be answered by such vague generalizations as those formulated by Graetz, whose standpoint is, as we have seen, adopted in all essentials by Dubnow.

It is true that the fundamental historiographical structure of Dubnow's great work appears to provide an implicit answer to some of these questions: in the first phases of Israel in Diaspora, the scattered communities were under the "hegemony" of the Oriental centers of both Palestine and Babylonia; in "the latter part of the Middle Ages" the hegemony was first of all Franco-Spanish and

then Spanish-German; the modern era—the expulsion
from Spain and the flowering of the autonomous center
in Poland—was the time of "the Ashkenazi hegemony";
and "the second phase of the modern era," the transitional
phase from the persecutions of 1648–49 to the partition of
Poland and the beginning of the *Haskalah* amongst the
Jews of western Europe, was the period of "Polish-German
hegemony."

But, in the actual contents of the work, Dubnow kept
to his "ground-plan" of chronological division by centers.
His strict adherence to this principle caused him to ob-
scure the inner unity of certain broad historical phenomena by breaking them up into isolated fragments, and
also led him into various inversions of the correct chronological sequence. We may illustrate "the break in historical continuity" resulting from Dubnow's method from
the part of his work dealing with the transitional phase of
the Diaspora.

Dubnow begins this "transitional phase," as already
noted, with the persecutions of 1648 and the messianic
"national movement" of Sabbatai Zevi. But the wildly
enthusiastic participation of the Sephardi communities in
this movement is not to be explained solely by the disas-
trous effect of these persecutions on the whole nation.
There is no doubt that other important factors were also
involved: the increasing power of the Spanish Inquisition,
which reached its height at that time (the reigns of
Philip III and Philip IV), the appalling regularity of
Jewish martydom, the existence of Jewish circles which
now had experience of secular authority and political
power (the Marranos), the impassioned homilies of Rabbi
Saul Morteira, and the veil of messianic mystery shroud-

42

ing the political activities of Menasseh ben Israel. All these developments not only gave a coloring of political realism to the yearnings for redemption and the messianic fantasies rife amongst the survivors of the Inquisition, but also provided Sabbatai Zevi's whole movement with the framework of a kind of state organization. Moreover, the close commercial and family ties binding together the widely scattered refugees from Spain and Portugal served as natural channels for the rapid transmission of the glad tidings of salvation and for the spread of the movement throughout the Diaspora. Hence, if Dubnow places his account of the scattered communities of Spanish Jewry (and also of Spinoza and Menasseh ben Israel) after the Baal Shem Tob and the Gaon of Vilna, after Mendelssohn and Joseph II (since "the centers of hegemony" have to be described first), it is clear that his conception of the Sabbatai Zevi movement must necessarily be very faulty.[44]

Now let us take an example of Dubnow's chronological inversions. His account of "the Jewish question in French literature" and of the "heralds of freedom" precedes "the return of the Jews to England" and "the controversy about the law of naturalization in England"; and only after all this does he come to a description of the condition of the Jews in Holland—for example, how the Dutch government protected the rights of Dutch Jews in Spain, thus indicating that the latter were officially recognized as naturalized Dutch citizens. Whereas the actual sequence of these events was, of course, the exact reverse of this: Holland, England, and then France! Instances of this kind could easily be multiplied: Mendelssohn before Spinoza, Weisl before M. H. Luzzatto, Solomon Maimon before Mendelssohn, etc.[45]

It must, furthermore, be remarked that several important historical phenomena which cannot be fitted into Dubnow's system (such as the *Yishuv* and immigration to Palestine) are completely ignored by the historian. These examples are, I think, sufficient to prove that Dubnow's historiographical analysis of the Diaspora by "the system of centers" not only fails to take account of the whole of Jewish history in that period, but also necessitates a departure from the fundamental principles of the correct writing of history.

XI

An important, and also partly new, contribution to the historical conception of Jewish life in the Dispersion was made by Eugen Taübler,[46] who starts from the assumption that the essential thing is "not to find the [pragmatic] connection between the extant records and other pieces of information [from the past], but to feel their historical content, to penetrate in some measure into the life processes which are reflected in them." Taübler's method is therefore inductive: instead of starting from the abstract concept of "the nation in the Diaspora," he studies the character of the various life processes that constitute the inner core of the concatenation of events.[47] On the basis of this inductive study, Taübler arrives at the conclusion that the principal and foremost life process in the history of Diaspora Judaism is the nation's physical and spiritual struggle with its alien environment: "The various manifestations of national life, which had once been held to-

44

gether and channeled into united action by the Jewish state, still strive to maintain themselves in being in the midst of other sovereign groupings. But since, in a new environment, they cannot preserve their original form and character, some of them change and some disappear. This is true of all the manifestations of national life, whether individual or public, in the religious and cultural sphere no less than in political, economic and social affairs."[48] Hence, Taübler's view of the relation of Diaspora history to general history is much closer to Jost's than to Graetz's:

> The fluctuating vicissitudes in the integration of the Jews into the German body politic were determined by the legal, economic and cultural conditions of the German people. These conditions were, in turn, very influential in bringing about the "inner change" in the national element in Judaism; and it is by their light that we must examine the influence exercised by the Jewish element in the population on the spiritual and social development of the German people. Insofar as the history of the Jews in Germany is concerned with matters of legal status or with economic questions and rights of residence, it is part of the general history of Germany, and this latter must therefore be made the basis of the study and exposition of Jewish history [in Germany]. Moreover "the internal history" of the Jews (their communal life, their reciprocal relations, the development of their religion, literature and customs) are not merely *subjected* to the continuous influence of the alien environment, but are actually *conditioned* by it: the legal system, economy, and general culture of the surrounding nations have all to be reckoned with as factors governing the development of the inner life of the Jews.[49]

Taübler does make a distinction between the local histories of the various different Diaspora communities and the general history of the Jews. But, whereas he explains the nature of the life-process which constitutes the history of every separate community, he does not do the same for the processes that unite the different parts of the dispersed nation into a single entity, and he thus gives us no clue to the real character of the "general history." Nor is that the only defect in his method. In another place, when analyzing the permanent processes of Jewish history, he divides them into the following categories: economic (migration and settlement); public (assimilation, individual and communal adaptation to the alien environment, the mutual relations between the Jews and the leading gentile citizens as reflected in the legal status of the Jews, in the influence exercised by them, and in the gentiles' opposition to this influence in all its forms, in anti-Semitism, etc.); and cultural (the "individuality" of the various communities, their internal organization and institutions, their mutual aid, their forms of divine worship and their reciprocal relations).[50] But here too he is mainly concerned with the definition of these processes as such, and does not explain the extent of their organic interconnection.

We see, then, that despite all the progress made in the systematic writing of Jewish history, there are still several fundamental historiographical questions which have not yet been properly clarified. No satisfactory analysis has yet been made of the extent to which the various Diaspora communities played an active part in the making of history, or of the nature and importance of the reciprocal influence exercised by these communities on each other, or even of the peculiarly spiritual character of Jewish history which almost all the historians more or less admit. Nor has the very nature of the unity which binds the scattered parts of the nation together into a single, historically significant entity yet been properly defined and explained. And the last of our questions, that about the part played by the Land of Israel in the history of the Diaspora, has, if the truth be told, hardly been dealt with at all.

XII

I therefore proceed to formulate my own replies to these questions:

1. *Even after the destruction of the Jewish state, when the homeless Jews were scattered amongst the nations and had been absorbed by the various states in which they lived, the unity of the Jewish people still remained complete and unbroken. Only the external conditions of the nation's existence changed, but not its essential character. Even in dispersion the nation formed a distinctive organic entity; that is to say, the various scattered Jewish communities were united by unique life processes which cannot be understood simply as the sum total of the lives of the individual members of the nation, or as the aggregate of the separate life processes of each single Diaspora community. The fundamental nature of this organic entity is not only socio-psychological, but also socio-political. In other words, its various parts are united into a single whole not only by a reciprocal psychological influence which is the source and mainstay of their emotional awareness of belonging to each other, but also by the close bonds forged in the struggle for survival which makes them present a*

united front to the outside world and sustains their politi-
cal will and their power of concerted action.

The socio-psychological feeling of unity springs from
the memories of a common past history and the consciousness of a common historical and cultural background. A
nation is like an individual. It is only the thread of the
individual's memories that constitutes his own personal
"ego" and unites his separate experiences into a single, integrated "psyche," so that if this thread of memories is
broken he loses his separate individuality and become
psychologically unbalanced. In the same way, the national
"ego" also depends on the thread of the memories shared
by all the nation, on the combination of thoughts and
community of feelings which are peculiar to the members
of that particular nation and which are bound up with
the events and experiences of their common past. Not
merely is it "incumbent on every Jew to regard himself as
having personally taken part in the Exodus from Egypt,"
but his memories of the past actually make him a partici-
pant not only in the Exodus, but also in all the important
events and decisive turning points in the nation's life.
Hence, the individual Jew's sense of national unity with
his fellow Jews is based on his awareness of their common
past. The events of the past are an inseparable part of the
national religious consciousness. Remnants of past history
have been embodied in certain national customs and beliefs and the impression made by past events has given
rise to the feeling of a common national destiny.

The socio-political feeling of unity springs from the living and deeply felt attachment to Palestine which nurtures
the active messianic hopes of the people and their longings for redemption, and also deepens their sense of "not

belonging" in the alien environment. This sense of "strangeness" is thus the source of the constant urge of the Diaspora communities to band themselves together in self-defense.

The socio-psychological awareness of national unity finds expression in "static" nationhood; that is to say, in cultural conditions common to all the dispersed Jewish communities, in the social and economic status of the Jews in the various lands of the Diaspora, in the Hebrew language (which was never completely dead, since it never ceased to perform socio-psychological functions in some particular community) and Jewish literature, in the Jewish household and Jewish domestic life, in forms of divine worship and religious ritual. The socio-political sense of unity, on the other hand, finds expression in "dynamic" nationhood; that is to say, in events resulting from the nation's capacity for concerted action—the waves of immigration to Palestine, the messianic movements, the social conflicts and the class struggle within the Jewish communities, the creation of forms of organization best suited to the unification and effective use of the nation's forces. But both these "static" and "dynamic" qualities of nationhood draw their being from the existence of the Jewish nation, which never ceased to be a single entity even in dispersion.

2. *Even in the days when they were an independent nation living in their own land the Jews were not "like all other peoples." The Jewish people were given a special national character and a special religious mission right from the beginning of their history. The traditional account of Abraham's departure from his home and of his*

subsequent choice by God is stamped with an unmistakably religious character.[51] *Equally unmistakable are the religious implications of the name "Israel," which denotes the special national character of the Jews. Similar implications are also preserved in the other personal names taken by Jews and in the numerous personal epithets and appellatives used by them. The historical significance of this is that the "social ties" which bound the "children of Israel" together into the "house of Israel" are seen to have resulted not only from public historical processes; they were also forged by the personal names chosen as a sign of their national identity by individual Jews who, out of their loyalty to the "God of Israel," banded themselves together into the "congregation of Israel" and the "community of Israel" and in every generation, in one form or another, now to a greater now to a lesser extent, pledged themselves "to keep and perform" the laws and statutes given to the Jewish people.*[52] *This religious element in Jewish nationhood gave a special aura of sanctity to the whole Jewish way of life and was one of the causes of the peculiar blend of religion and nationalism in Judaism. The extent to which these two elements were harmoniously fused together differed from generation to generation, since there was naturally a constant struggle between them for the dominant role in the molding of the nation's life. This tension and conflict are an essential part of Jewish history at all times, including the Diaspora period. True, the cessation of the nation's political life and its exile from its own land increased the importance of the part played by the religious element, but they did not put an end to the continued existence of the national and secular element. In this respect too the history of Jews in Diaspora is a di-*

rect continuation of the history of the Jews in their own land, although it follows different channels.

3. The limits of both the "static" and the "dynamic" nationhood of Diaspora Judaism are determined by the ethnic character, the social order and economic system, and the political and administrative organization of the countries in which the various parts of the nation were dispersed, and also by the civic and cultural condition of the peoples in whose midst the Jews resided. All these factors together constituted the framework within which —and only within which—the vital forces of the nation were given a chance to create and act, to organize themselves and come to terms with their environment.

The Arabs, for example, treated the "heretics" with tolerance and even permitted them a large degree of autonomy. The Jews in Islamic lands were thus able to take advantage of the religious toleration accorded them to create organs of self-government. But the social and political status of the Jews under the caliphate, and the character, form and organization of Jewish autonomy (with the exilarchate corresponding to the former monarchy, and the sages to the former priesthood, etc.), were a purely Jewish development resulting from the inner dynamism of Jewish nationhood. Within the historical framework of the rise of the feudal system the Jews were in need of special protection by the authorities in the form of "charters"; but the legal contents and scope of these "charters" resulted from the concerted action of the Jewish communities in the lands of Christendom. The political framework created by the constant struggle in Spain between the Arab and Berber elements of the population made it possible for the Jews to take an active and large part in Spanish political life. But it did not dictate either the extent or the form of this participation, both of which are to be explained only by the interplay of the inner forces in Spanish Jewry. Obviously, the framework within which the Jews live does not remain the same in all periods, but constantly changes, expanding or contracting, in the course of history. However, its degree of stability depends on factors entirely outside the sphere of Jewish history. As long as the framework remains fixed, the Jewish life inside it also preserves a steady regularity: the dynamic forces of the nation are denied an outlet and only its static socio-psychological qualities find expression in firmly rooted cultural traditions and stable ways of life. Hence periods of general political stability are times when the scattered communities of the Diaspora can consolidate their positions in their countries of residence.

But in periods of general crisis and upheaval, when tremendous revolutionary changes occur in the alignment of the forces constituting the outer framework of Jewish life, the dynamic forces of Jewish nationhood break out from their confinement, throw off the chains of the established order and the fetters of a time-honored tradition, and strive to shape their own destiny. In most cases they also enter the arena of the general political struggle, in one form or another—sometimes by voluntary choice and sometimes by instinctive compulsion, sometimes with passionate fervour and sometimes with timid hesitancy. This step is usually forced upon the Jews by the nature of the historical events. In times of revolutionary ferment there is usually a violent eruption of the pent-up anti-Jewish emotions that have accumulated in various circles of the indigenous population during the preceding period of stability. The former fixed and agreed framework within which the Jews could live their lives in peace and security now disintegrates into a lawless anarchy in which they are exposed to wanton attacks and are obliged to band together in self-defense. Periods of political revolution, national migrations and ideological conflicts are thus critical times in the history of the Jewish Diaspora.[53]

Epochal changes in general history must, therefore, of necessity bring about fundamental changes in Jewish life. A new era in general history heralds a new era of Jewish history in the Diaspora.

But epochal historical changes do not long remain confined within the borders of a single country, nor can the rise, existence and fall of regimes be insulated within a single nation. The Arab conquests and the emergence of the feudal system in Europe, the Crusades and the struggle between the Church and the Roman Empire, the rise of the medieval cities and the coming into being of the new empires, the Reformation and the great voyages of discovery, the French Revolution and modern democracy—all these decisive and epoch-making historical developments affected, to a greater or lesser extent, practically all the countries where Jews were living. For this reason, both the periods of stability and the periods of crisis in the history of the Diaspora were never confined to a single country, but were always the common lot of all the scattered Jewish communities.

4. It is certainly true that the various Diaspora communities were not of equal historical significance. It is also correct to maintain, as Dubnow did, that those com-

munities "which were distinguished by the greater intensity of their inner life" dominated the others; and it is perhaps possible, with certain reservations, to call the dominant community "a center" in relation to those dominated by it, especially if the community in question was large in numbers and thus constituted, quantatively as well as qualitatively, a considerable part of the whole nation.

At the same time, however, a careful distinction must be made between a "center" of authority and a "center" of influence, that is, between a community connected with all the others by certain organizational ties and unquestioningly accepted by them as their authority in religious matters, and a community that, while not connected with the rest of the Diaspora by any such organizational ties, has, in consequence of certain historical circumstances, come to serve as a social and cultural model to all the other communities which copy its example for a certain period of time.

Such a "center of authority" was Palestinian Jewry. All the communities of the Diaspora were dependent on it in such religious matters as the exact dates of the festivals and the intercalation of the year, and it maintained regular contact with them all through "the emissaries of Zion" and "the pilgrims." Moreover, there was the great prestige of the land of Palestine as such, deriving from the ancient traditions of its religious sanctity. Babylonian Jewry was also, in some measure, a "center of authority" enjoying a position of unquestioned preeminence due to its highly organized religious and national autonomy, which rested both on a hallowed religious tradition (the Talmud) and on permanent and frequent religious and cultural contacts with the other communities of the Diaspora (the *yeshiv-oth* and their organization). But all the other centers listed by Dubnow were only "centers of influence," the true nature of which cannot be properly understood without a preliminary examination of the reciprocal influence exerted by the communities of the Diaspora on each other.

We have already seen that the unity of the nation was, throughout the period of the Diaspora, fostered by the special way of life which was common to all the scattered communities and which at all times found concrete expression in all the various forms and manifestations of the nation's creative spirit: its faith and religion, its language and literature, its customs and manners, its institutions and organizations, its trends and movements. Although this creativeness was shared alike by all the communities of the Diaspora, of whose lives it was the authentic expression, it nevertheless originated primarily in those lands in which the real tendency and true character of the given historical period—whether it was to be one of stability or one of crisis—were most clearly evident. Hence every period had its own particular "centers of influence." In periods of stability, when the socio-psychological elements of the nation's unity are most prominent, the degree of influence exercised by the Jewish communities depends on the extent to which they are able to consolidate their own positions and integrate themselves into the foreign nation-states, and on their readiness to adapt themselves to their environment and give up their own distinctive individuality. This influence stands in direct relation to the stability of these communities and in inverse proportion to their adaptation to their environment (Babylonia, Spain, and Germany in the 19th century). Conversely, in periods of crisis, when the socio-political elements of the nation's unity come to the fore, the permanent influence of the communities is in inverse proportion to the extent of the crisis[54] and in direct relation to the strength of their political will and their capacity for concerted action (France and Germany at the time of the Crusades, Russia during the years 1878–1914, and America today).

5. *The unity of the Jewish nation in exile and dispersion was also the organized unity of a people living according to laws, customs and practices of its own which regulated every aspect of public and private life to an extent that can hardly be paralleled even in the most highly organized states. The main importance of this does not lie in the fact that the Jews in certain countries were granted the "privilege" of being subject only to their own laws. What is still more significant is that the organization of the nation's autonomy was founded on a complete set of beliefs and ideas, a "comprehensive ideology," which provided the basis for the individual Jew's readiness to observe these laws and to obey the authorities appointed in every community to guard the laws and customs of the whole nation. This "ideology" is therefore, by its very nature, one of the "spiritual" phenomena in the life of Jewry in the Diaspora.*

6. *It is thus clear that the record of the various manifestations of the nation's spirit must occupy a larger place in the history of the Jews than in that of all other peoples. Even the socio-political element in the unity of the dispersed nation more often manifested itself as a desire or aspiration, a trend of thought or visionary movement, than in the form of concerted and militant action. This does*

not mean, however, that in writing Jewish history all we
have to do is to give an account of the philosophical systems of the Jewish sages or a literary appreciation of Jewish poetry. These are matters for students of the history
of philosophy or for the historians of Hebrew literature.
The writer of Jewish history must deal with the manifestations of the nation's spirit, insofar as they became part
of the soul of the average, ordinary Jew who carried on
the tradition of the special way of life shared in common
by all the communities of the Diaspora. The whole spiritual character of any given generation is determined by this
historically anonymous "average" Jew's view of life, his
beliefs and opinions, his ways of thought and manners of
expression, his emotions and dreams. It is by the width of
the gap separating "popular beliefs" from "philosophical
views"—the former "static" and the latter "dynamic"—
that the spiritual character of the "average" Jew in every
generation is to be determined; and the record of the
variations in this gap from one generation to another
constitutes the spiritual history of the whole nation. From
this point of view the historian is more interested in the
questions asked by Jewish philosophy than in its answers;
and the methods by which it arrives at its conclusions are
for him more important than the conclusions themselves.
Similarly, in dealing with Jewish poetry, the historian must
be more concerned with the poet's themes than with his
beliefs; and in discussing the latter he must pay more attention to the character of the poet's symbols than to the
artistic perfection of his imagery. The questions asked by
Jewish philosophy and the methods by which it attempts
to find an answer to them reflect the doubts and uncer-
tainties, the intellectual conflicts and dilemmas of the

generation in question, the themes and symbols of Jewish poetry its cares and joys, its dreams and struggles.

7. *Even during the period of the Diaspora, the Land of Israel and its Jewish population still played a part of general importance in the history of the nation. Nor was this only because the deep and continuing emotional influence of the past, and the longings for redemption that fortified the nation's spirit in times of oppression and persecution, were all inseparably connected with Palestine which still remained the Holy Land. The special importance of the Land of Israel in the period of the Diaspora was also a consequence of the unique position, historically and territorially, occupied by the* Yishuv *among the dispersed Jewish communities.*[55] *This uniqueness of the* Yishuv *resulted from three basic facts: its historical continuity, its individual character, and its complete Jewishness.*

(a) Its historical continuity. *There never ceased to be a Jewish population in Palestine. Till the time of the Crusades it was very numerous; and even the wars of the Crusades, which resulted in the wholesale destruction of Jewish communities in Palestine, did not put an end to its continuity. The* Yishuv *continued to exist, and life returned to the devastated communities after a short time. This historical continuity made itself felt in many fields: in the durability of the* Yishuv's *religious tradition, despite the frequent changes in the composition of the* Yishuv *caused by waves of immigration; in the permanence of its forms of organization, despite the succession of foreign overlords; in its religious authority over the whole of Jewry, in spite of opposition from without and dissension from within; and in its high level of Jewish culture, in spite of the harsh material conditions of its existence and its very limited chances of social development, both of which might have been expected greatly to reduce its cultural level.*

For many generations—down to the Crusades—the office of *Nasi* (Patriarch) continued to exist as part of the *Yishuv's* political organization. The *Nasi* preserved his full rights and status as at once the supreme authority in religious matters, the recognized national representative in dealings with foreign powers, the official leader of the Jewish community, the highest legal authority, the head of the Great *Yeshivah*, and also as the "surviving descendant" of the house of David. Even many generations after the Crusades several attempts were made, in various ways, to restore the "hegemony" of Palestine. This historical continuity was also largely responsible for the cultural continuity of the *Yishuv*, which was most strikingly demonstrated in the community's knowledge of the Law and in the extent of its use of the Hebrew language.

(b) The individual character of the Yishuv. *In almost every period of the Diaspora, the Jewish population of Palestine was dependent on the Jewish communities dispersed in other lands. The constant financial assistance given to the* Yishuv *by these communities was at all times an organic—and most important—part of the economic realities of Jewish life in Palestine. Indeed, the Jewish population in Palestine depended on the Diaspora for its actual physical survival. By ensuring a steady flow of Jews to Palestine, the successive waves of immigration made good the "population deficit" caused in every generation*

by the harsh conditions of life in the country and by emigration, which was just as constant as the reverse process, although, of course, to take a well known example, the immigration of the three hundred rabbis was noised abroad far more than the emigration of their sons. Politically too the Yishuv was always in need of the protection of the Diaspora. In times of grave crisis the persistent representations made by the Jewish communities in Cairo and Constantinople—and later also in the European capitals— would result in the central authorities' intervening to save the Yishuv from its numerous enemies. This assistance from the Diaspora—in the form of a steady supply of new immigrants and constant financial and political support— was thus essential to the very existence of the Jewish population in Palestine, but also made it largely independent of the local conditions of the country. The small, devastated and impoverished state could not support an urban population of any numerical importance. At the same time, the prevailing political and administrative circumstances made it impossible to establish any Jewish agriculture or to set up Jewish industries and crafts on any serious scale, although several important attempts were made to do both. All this means that, historically speaking, the Yishuv was not just a "relic" which had survived by force of historical inertia, but neither did it resemble any of the Jewish communities of the Diaspora which were equipped by their local conditions to absorb and settle Jewish migrants. The whole existence of the Yishuv was something sui generis *resulting entirely from a ceaseless, generations-long struggle, carried on by the whole of Jewry, and from the repeated and constant efforts made by unknown individuals and organized groups who, by their unflagging determination, kept the* Yishuv *in being, despite all obstacles and in the face of all attacks. They saved the Land from being abandoned by Jews, they preserved its congregations from complete destruction, and they ensured that the Law should not be forgotten in the Land and that the return to Zion should still be fervently prayed for. The organization, scope and effectiveness of these efforts were subject, it is true, to the actual conditions of political rule prevailing in Palestine at any given time; but the efforts as such were entirely independent of these external factors and depended solely on the Jewish people and the relations existing between it and its land.*

It is in this respect that the *Yishuv* was unique. In no other land, throughout all the phases of the Diaspora, was there a Jewish community whose existence was, to such an extent, the result of an individual spiritual effort maintained for generations. From this standpoint it makes no difference which of the various sects contributed most to keeping the Jewish population of Palestine in existence and even to increasing its numbers—the "mourners of Zion" or the messianic visionaries, those who "waited hopefully for the redemption" or "the keepers of the walls," Rabbinists or Karaites, *Hassidim* or *Mitnaggedim*, and the like. What was common to all these groups was the effort made by numerous individual Jews not merely to preserve, but also to enhance, the special way of life of the *Yishuv*, an effort stimulated by the inner forces of the nation, and not by any favorable outward circumstances of the country itself.

(c) The complete Jewishness of the Yishuv. *The Jewish population in Palestine was the element of the nation that remained most uncompromisingly and stubbornly loyal to its Jewish heritage. Hence the strongest forces in Judaism from all the lands of the Diaspora were at all times drawn to Palestine—starting with such men as Judah Halevi and Jonathan of Lunel, Shimshon of Sens and Yehiel of Paris, the Ramban and his disciples. Ishtori Ha-Parhi and Obadiah of Bertinoro, Isaac Luria and Joseph Caro, Moses Cordovero and Isaiah Horowitz (the author of* The Two Tablets of the Law), *and continuing right down to Hayyim ben Atar, the followers of the Baal Shem Tob and the pupils of the Gaon of Vilna, the orthodox Jews of Hungary and the Lithuanian* Mitnaggedim. *All these, and many others, by doing their creative work in Palestine, or continuing it there, helped to make the country into a center of intensive Jewish life.*

The Land of Israel and its Jewish population are thus seen to be an intrinsic part of Jewish history in the Diaspora, and not just loosely connected with it by their association with the nation's past memories and future hopes. The *Yishuv,* as already stated, exercised a magnetic attraction on all those forces in Judaism that were bent on preserving the independence of the Jewish way of life and its historical continuity. The close connection between the *Yishuv,* on the one hand, and the waves of immigration and the constantly recurring messianic ferments, on the other, was a natural consequence of the character of the *Yishuv.* In periods when the influence of the *Yishuv* on the life of the whole nation was in the ascendancy, there was a corresponding rise in the intensity of Jewish life everywhere. The strength of this influence is not to be measured by the number of Jews living in Palestine, but rather by the inner character of the *Yishuv*—by the completeness and intensity of its Jewishness. Geographically, Palestine was part of the Near Eastern dominions, first of the Mamelukes and then of the Turks, and this geopolitical situation undoubtedly determined the external framework of Jewish life in the country. But historically speaking—in terms of the *Yishuv's* influence and its connection with Jewish history as a whole—its place in every period is in the heart of the Jewish struggle for survival, as the center of "Jewish intensity" and "Jewish stubbornness" in every generation.

XIII

On the basis of what has been said above, it seems to me that the main events in the history of Diaspora Judaism fall into three separate and parallel, though also interconnected and partly interdependent, groups: (1) the status of the Jews in the various lands of the Diaspora; (2) Jewish communal activity, especially in those countries where the Jewish population was most numerous and best organized; and (3) the world and work of the individual Jew. These three main categories, with all their numerous subdivisions and all the various shifts and changes that occurred within each of them from one generation to another, comprise the whole contents of the history of the Jews as a dispersed and oppressed people.

(1) The status of the Jews in the various lands of the Diaspora. *This historical category may be subdivided as follows: the political, legal and social status of the Jews in*

63

their countries of residence; Jewish participation in, and influence on, the political and social life of these countries; the number, population and location of the Jewish settlements and congregations and their relative density; the economic activity and importance of the Jews; their standard of living and social image. The condition of Palestine and its Jewish population in every period are also an essential factor in determining the general status of the Jews in that period. This status, and the changes that occurred in it from one generation to another, are conditioned by the general history of the period in question.

(2) Jewish communal activity. *Here the subdivisions are: the social ferments and the religio-messianic movements, widely different in their tendencies and aims, which were, at all times and in all places, a constantly recurring feature of Judaism in the Diaspora; "the centers of Jewry," with their communities and institutions, the religious reforms of their sages, and the part played by them in moulding the character of the Jewish public.*

(3) The world of the individual Jew *comprises the following subdivisions: domestic manners and family customs, mourning rites and forms of joyful celebration, rules of etiquette and proper conduct, types of Sabbath and festival observance, popular beliefs and religious philosophies, the basic tenets of Judaism, the service of the synagogue, religious rituals and forms of divine worship, the languages spoken and written by Jews, and educational methods. Also included under this general heading is the whole creative activity of the nation's spirit in the fields of religious and secular knowledge, scientific study and research, poetry and literature, and the extent to which this cre-*

*ativeness spread to and influenced the various circles of
the whole nation. And, of course, here too belongs the
part played by the Jews in furthering the progress of
the sciences in their countries of residence.*

The character of the different periods in the history of
the Diaspora is determined by the combination of these
three categories of events and the constantly changing
"historical type" created by them. Each period is marked
off from the others by the special status of the Jews in it,
by its own particular movements and ferments, centers
and institutions, religious reforms and decrees, and by the
distinctive character of its individual Jew and its "historical type."

However, although the new features of each particular
period are revealed to us in all three of the above historical
categories, there must and can be only one starting point
in any attempt to draw chronological dividing lines—
namely, *the changes that occurred in the status of the
Jews.* These changes are an outcome of the general historical framework of the period and are felt by the people
of the time in terms of changed conditions of life through
which they become aware that they are standing at a
turning-point of history and on the threshold of a new
era. This contemporary awareness is actually one of the
"objective data" which the historian must take into account when determining the beginning of every new
historical period.

In the history of Diaspora Judaism we can distinguish
eight such turning points: the Arab conquests; the persecutions of the Jews at the beginning of the Crusades; the
Lateran Council (which laid down the political policy of

the Catholic Church with regard to the Jews); the "Black Death"; the expulsion from Spain and Portugal; the Chmelnicky massacres; the first Emancipation at the time of the French Revolution; and the pogroms in Russia in the early eighties of the last century. Every one of these turning points produced a change in the status of the Jews, and it was this change that determined the basic character of the period of Jewish history immediately following.

XIV

The history of Diaspora Judaism is accordingly to be divided into the following eight periods:

(1) The first period of stability, *embracing both the Oriental and the Occidental Diaspora communities, the former of which consolidated their positions in this period, while the latter began to establish themselves. The period begins with the Arab conquests and ends with the First Crusade (636–1096). Its general framework is formed by the social, political and cultural unification of the new forces that now rose to world power by conquest (Islam and the caliphates in the East, the Church and the Holy Roman Empire in the West). As far as the status of the Jews is concerned, the fundamental characteristic of the period is the active part played by the Jews in the processes that led to the emergence of these new forces: in the establishment of new centers of population and in the building of new cities, in the organization of the national*

economies and of international trade, in diplomacy and in the development of international communications, in the workings of governmental administration and in the progress of the sciences. Under the heading of Jewish status in this period, we must also include the driving out of the Jewish population of Palestine from its own land and the Arabization of the country. As regards the activity of world Jewry, the distinctive features of this period are the concentration of large numbers of Jews in Islamic lands and the organization of the whole of Jewry under an accepted and recognized leadership (exilarchs and princes, geonim *and* yeshivoth) *which held together the scattered communities by spreading the knowledge of the Talmud and establishing the absolute religious authority of that work, and by strongly opposing the widespread popular tendencies which found expression in social ferment and messianic movements, in dissident sects and violent religious polemics. As regards the world of the individual Jew, this period saw the final codification of the Jewish way of life, based on the acceptance of the Babylonian Talmud together with a certain measure of adaptation to the conditions of the new environment (the reforms introduced by the* geonim *and by Rabbenu Gershom, and by others). In addition, this was the period of the first awakenings of Jewish critical thought and research, stimulated by closer contact with other societies in whose formation the Jews were driven by the force of historical circumstances to take an active part.*

(2) The first period of crisis, again embracing the whole of Jewry, when the position of the Jews in all the lands of the Diaspora was gravely undermined. This

period begins with the persecutions of the Crusades, and ends with the decrees of Pope Innocent III and the resolutions of the fourth Lateran Council defining the status of the Jews in Christian lands (1096–1215). Its general framework: the wars between Orient and Occident (the Crusades in the East and the struggle between Moslems and Christians in Spain), and the quarrel between the Holy Roman Empire and the Church. From the standpoint of Jewish status in the Diaspora, the fundamental feature of this period is the destruction of the hitherto existing bases of Jewish existence: Jewish life and property were no longer secure; the Jews were exposed to murderous attacks by incited mobs; charge after charge of ritual murder was brought against them solely for the purpose of justifying these acts of murder and pillage; and they were subjected to various methods of religious coercion, while they, for their part, made desperate attempts to find some protection and shelter from their tormentors. As regards the activity of world Jewry, the distinctive characteristics of the period are the weakening of the ties between the Jewish communities in Islamic lands and those in western countries, the disappearance of any organized leadership of world Jewry, and the rise of the European Jewish communities, especially those of Spain, France and Germany. The one generally recognized and accepted supreme authority in Jewry was gradually replaced by the systematic work done by individual sages and whole congregations in organizing Jewish life and adapting it to the new conditions, and in strengthening Judaism from within so that it could survive centuries of oppression (Maimonides). The "climate" of Jewish communal activity in this period was one of intense religious messianic ferment which affected the whole of Jewry and left a deep impres-

sion both on Jewish public life and on the world of the individual Jew. Hence, where the character of the individual Jew is concerned, this period marks the beginning both of the conception of martyrdom as the guiding principle of a pious Jewish life lived in accordance with the precepts of the Law, and also of the growth of the mystic trends in Jewish religious life and thought.

(3)   The second period of stability, *stability in servitude —from the decrees of Innocent III to the "Black Death" (1215–1348). The general framework of this period: the rule of the Catholic Church and the Pope in the West and the growth of religious fanaticism in the lands of Islam. From the standpoint of Jewish status, this was a period when the Jews could ensure their survival only by submitting to becoming the slaves of their overlords. The Jews were literally the chattels of the Emperor who could "hand them over" to others, "forgo" them, and even mortgage them; special taxes were imposed on them; they were forced to observe the Jew-laws of the Church, and so on. However, this servile status did not prevent some Jews from playing a noticeable part in the national economies of their countries of residence in this period too, so much so that there was in fact a glaring contrast between the "stability in servitude" of the Jewish population as a whole and the actual positions occupied by certain strata of Jews in the life of the nation and country in which they lived. This contrast was one of the causes of the bloody final chapter of the period which closed with the massacres set off by the "Black Death." From the standpoint of world Jewry the salient fact in this period is the destruction of the Oriental centers of Jewish life. Most of the great Jewish communities and congregations in the*

lands of Islam were so decimated by the Crusades and by the devastations of the Mongol hordes that, for long afterwards, they virtually ceased to play any part in Jewish history. At this same time, western Jewry was embroiled in the spiritual struggle between the protagonists of "Arabic learning" and rationalistic philosophy, on the one hand, and the adherents of cabbalistic mysticism, on the other. The literary polemics with which this public debate was conducted left their mark on Jewish communal activity in this period, particularly on its two main centers in Spain and France. As regards the world of the individual Jew, this period saw a further strengthening of those trends toward pietism, asceticism and the formation of dissident sects which had first appeared in the previous period.

(4) The second period of crisis, the period of the wholesale destruction of Jewish communities. This begins with the "Black Death," during which practically the whole of German Jewry and part of the Jewish communities in other countries of Europe were wiped out, and ends with the expulsion from Spain and Portugal which extinguished the once glorious light of Spanish Jewry and dispersed its survivors and their descendants over many countries (1348–1496). The general framework of this period: the decay of Papal rule and the decline of the Holy Roman Empire in the West, the life-and-death struggle of these two crumbling powers against the new forces emerging within their borders (confederacies of cities, the spread of heresy, new states), and the renewal of the war between East and West (Spain against the remnants of the Moors, the Byzantine Empire against the Turks).

From the standpoint of Jewish status, the fundamental feature of this period is the general determined effort to put an end to the existence of the Jews, whether by forced conversions (the representatives of the Church), or by the expulsion of the Jewish population and the confiscation of their property (the kings), or by mass killings of Jews in order to get rid of economic rivals and expropriate their possessions (the cities and the incited mobs). As regards the activity of world Jewry, this was a period in which the nation was, so to speak, paralyzed. Generations of persecution and forced conversion in Spain deprived Jewry of many of its most active intellectual forces and greatly depleted the class from which its communal leaders and spiritual guides were drawn. The expulsion from France ruined and dispersed one of the most active of all the medieval Jewish communities. Of German Jewry there remained only a few remnants which here and there managed to revive some sort of organized Jewish life. World Jewry was thus spiritually paralyzed too. Altogether, this period was the nadir of Jewish life, unredeemed by any social awakening or religious ferment. The Jews of this period devoted their energies primarily to the preservation and careful recording of Jewish customs, to the punctilious observance of the practical commandments (mitzvot), and to their increasingly rigorous imposition as a preparation for the steadfast endurance of persecution. The world of the individual Jew also appears at its most wretched in this period—a world of religious martyrs whose life was one long preparation for death.

(5) The third period of stability, when the Jews were officially "protected." This lasts from the expulsion of the

Jews from Spain and Portugal down to the Chmelnicky massacres of 1648, the destruction of Ukrainian Jewry and the beginning of the decline of the Jewish communities in Turkey and Poland. The general framework of the period: the wars of religion in Europe (the Reformation and the emergence of secular states no longer dominated by the Catholic Church) and the rising power of Turkey, Poland and Holland. From the standpoint of Jewish status, the period is characterized by the mass concentration of Jews in the lands in which they enjoyed the "protection" of the secular authorities (Turkey and Poland), the first recognition of the principle of religious toleration with regard to the Jews (Holland), and the active participation of the Jews in the economic life of their countries of residence. In terms of the activity of world Jewry, the distinctive features of the period are: the close ties between the Jewish communities in different countries, resulting from the dispersion of the Spanish and Portugese exiles who played a major part in the creation of "one Jewish world" in this period; the emergence, in various states, of a class of influential Jews who were able once more to use their power of intercession, in both old and new ways, with the non-Jewish authorities; the organization of Polish Jewry on an autonomous basis with its own central institutions, which made it an influential factor in Jewish life everywhere; and the rise of Palestine, and particularly Safed, as the center of the religious ferment in Judaism (Isaac Luria and the Cabbalah) the effects of which radiated throughout the Diaspora. All these developments also nurtured the eager messianic hopes and tense expectancy of redemption that were typical of this time. The world of the individual Jew in this period is characterized, above all, by its variety of

72

conflicting and contrasting facets (talmudic orthodoxy in Poland, "enlightened" skepticism in Italy, and visionary mysticism in Palestine and the Orient generally), and by the harmonization of all these different elements by the messianic dynamism of the Cabbalah into a new and ecstatic Jewish way of life to which it gave its own individual expression in Hebrew literature.

(6)   The third period of crisis, *the crisis of inner decay, from the Chmelnicky massacres down to the French Revolution (1648–1789). The general framework of the period: the decline of the feudal states (Poland and Turkey) and the rise of autocratic regimes based on a bureaucratic administration, feudal privileges for the aristocracy, and economic incentives for the rising class of the bourgeoisie. From the standpoint of Jewish status, the fundamental characteristic of the period is the growing insecurity, economic impoverishment, and social decline of the Jewish masses in the countries where the Jewish population was densest (Poland and Turkey), in contrast to the increasing security and the political, economic and social integration of the relatively small number of Jews in the emergent states. As regards the activity of world Jewry, the distinctive features of this period are the dispersion of the main concentrations of Jews and the decline of their communal organizations, the weakening of Jewish autonomy and the growth of new organizational forms arising from popular movements which embraced the whole of Jewry (the Sabbatai Zevi ferment and its aftermaths, the beginning of Hassidism and of the Haskalah). The world of the individual Jew in this period is characterized by inner disintegration and impoverishment.*

(7) The fourth period of stability *the period of natu-ralization and emancipation, from the French Revolution to the pogroms of the eighties in Russia (1789–1881).*[56] *The general framework of the period: the economic de-velopment of the countries of Europe by a policy of* laissez faire, *the growth of social and cultural equality, the strengthening of national consciousness and unity, and the development of democratic regimes.*

From the standpoint of Jewish status, the fundamental feature of the period is the active part played by the Jews in all the above processes, in consequence of an ever in-creasing degree of economic and territorial integration, cultural and social assimilation, and political emancipa-tion. The distinctive features of world Jewish activity are to be found, first of all, in the various contradictions and contrasts that now made themselves felt in the whole fabric of world Jewry. On the one hand, this was weakened by the processes of social disintegration and cultural as-similation, and by the repudiation of Jewish nationhood and the contraction of Jewish religion; but, at the same time, it was strengthened by the rise of the populous and densely concentrated Russian Jewish community and the emergence of many large Jewish congregations in all the countries of Europe, by the development of Jewish his-torical consciousness and the growing sense of a common Jewish destiny, and by the new possibilities of mutual aid opened up to world Jewry by the special forms of organi-zation that had come into being in the democratic states. The movement for religious reform and the opposition to it, the joint Jewish struggle for equal rights, and the vari-ous national and international Jewish organizations all made the activity of "world Jewry" an important factor in Jewish life in this period, and set the stage for the new prophets of the Return to Zion. The world of the individual Jew in this period was characterized by the difference which now made itself felt between the Jewish communities of western and eastern Europe. In the West, the processes of cultural assimilation and religious adaptation led to a narrowing down of the specifically Jewish content of the individual Jew's life, and consequently to a weakening of his peculiarly Jewish image. Not so in eastern Europe, with its densely populated Jewish communities which had their own distinctive way of life and their own deeply rooted Jewish cultural traditions. There, only a thin stratum of the Jewish population was affected by the processes of civil and political emancipation and of social and cultural assimilation; though, at the same time, large scale efforts were made to promote the territorial and economic integration of the Jews and their spiritual awakening. In the character of the individual eastern European Jew there was thus a blending of the old and the new which is reflected in the revived Hebrew language of the *Haskalah* literature.[57]

(8) The fourth period of crisis, *a period of constant attacks on the Jews aimed at their total exclusion from non-Jewish society. The period begins with the rise of anti-Semitism in Germany and the pogroms in Russia, and ends with the establishment of the State of Israel (1881–1948). Its general historical framework is the strengthening of national and social elements in the various states, and the growing intensity of the struggle for power against the background of a world torn by class conflicts, party strife, international quarrels and wars, and great power rivalries.*

As regards Jewish status, this period is distinguished by

the ruthless *physical* onslaught on the Jews, which was encouraged by organized mass-incitement as part of a deliberate political and social policy, and which culminated, after the rise to power of the Nazis, in the destruction of European Jewry and the extermination of six million Jews. The outstanding feature of world Jewish activity in this period is the re-unification of the Jews into a single political and national group living in its own land and speaking its own language, a development which was brought about by the political revolt of the Jewish masses and their organization for self-defense, and by the growing power of Jewish nationalism. These processes resulted in the migration of millions of Jews and the establishment of new centers of Jewish population, in the political, national and social awakening of the Jewish masses, and in the setting up of world-wide Jewish organizations for mutual aid and protection and for the resettlement and political revival of the nation in its own land. The world of the individual Jew in this period was characterized by the recovery of its inner unity, and by the new sense of Jewish pride and independence which developed side by side with the processes of revolt, self-defense and growing national strength. The emergence of a new type of Jew is reflected in the revival of the Hebrew language and of Hebrew literature, in the rise of Yiddish, and in the renascence of Hebrew and Jewish culture.

BOOK

II

THE MODERN PERIOD

I

The terms "recent generations" or "modern times" are commonly employed to denote the period of history which is close to us not only in time, but also in character—in its material circumstances, philosophical outlook, and general view of life. The problems which exercised the people of that period, the goals which they set themselves and the methods by which they sought to attain them, are all readily intelligible to us, precisely because they are so similar to our own views, aspirations, and ways of action. That is why the history of these recent generations can truly be called modern history, since in them the past imperceptibly merges with the present by the very nature of the historical circumstances.[1] However, when it comes to determining the beginning of modern Jewish history, we find that scholarly opinion is divided. Until very recently, the generally accepted theories of Jewish historiographers on "modern times" in Jewish history were based on the views of Graetz and Dubnow, both as explicitly expressed in the remarks of these historians on these times[2] and as evident in the general historiographical structure of their works,[3] and also as implied by the whole tenor of their writing about this period.[4] Some scholars adopted Graetz's method and began the modern period of Jewish history from the second half of the eighteenth century (1750),[5] while others followed Dubnow in dating the beginning of this period to the time of the French Revolution at the end of the eighteenth century (1789).[6] The difference between these two views stems from two different estimates of the character of "the new type of Jew." Was he the Europeanized Jewish intellectual with

79

the new modern outlook or the recently emancipated citizen whose equal status was officially recognized by the state? The year 1750 is the date of one of the first public manifestations of the *Haskalah*, the Enlightenment movement associated with the name of Moses Mendelssohn: in this year Mendelssohn started to publish, in Berlin, the Hebrew journal *Kehillat Musar*, in which he proclaimed the need for the cultural enlightenment of the Jewish masses. To Graetz's way of thinking, the character of modern Jewish life has been determined, in the main, by the *Haskalah* movement, which, in the lifetime of its most important representative, also became a kind of symbol of the whole course of Jewish history in recent times as a steady, continuous ascent from humiliation and degradation to that self-recognition and self-respect the growth of which characterizes the fourth and latest phase in Jewish history[7] (the preceding three being the time of the First Temple, the time of the Second Temple, and the period from the destruction of the Second Temple down to 1750).[8] This "self-recognition" found expression in two great movements which have together determined the character of "modern" Jewish history: "Enlightenment" and "Emancipation."

Of these two, the Enlightenment was first in time and importance. *Haskalah* was not only a matter of the Jews' adopting the languages of the states under whose rule they happened to be living and of the peoples in whose midst they dwelt, nor yet of their acquiring the modern culture which enabled them to meet their antagonists on equal terms. Historically speaking, *Haskalah* was essentially a process of inner liberation and spiritual purification from which resulted all the achievements of Jewry in the

80

fields of education and teaching, science and literature, social organization and religious reform. All the changes that occurred in the inner life of the Jews were inseparably bound up with the various aspects of the growth of Jewish self-recognition and self-respect—in the emergence of free thought and the awakening of scientific criticism, the widening of general knowledge and the development of Jewish studies, the aesthetic quest to improve taste and style and the attempts made by a rationalistic theology to modernize the forms of divine worship. Emancipation itself was also an outcome of a form of recognition—the gentiles' legal and social recognition of Jewish equality.[9] This recognition enabled the Jews to develop their potential powers and to enter fully into the economic, cultural, social and political life of the gentile nations. The phase of growing Jewish self-knowledge thus begins with Mendelssohn's first public activities.

In the opinion of other scholars, however, Emancipation is the decisive fact in modern Jewish history. It was the new social status of the Jews that determined both the content and scope of modern Jewish life and the mutual relations, based on joint participation in the cultural and civic fields, which now developed between Jews and non-Jews; and it was this status that also changed the direction of the individual Jew's way of thinking and the content of his intellectual awareness, by releasing him from the confines of his own narrow world and making him a citizen of modern European culture. On this view, too, the character of modern Jewry has been determined by two movements: the one for emancipation, including all the efforts made by the Jews in modern times to obtain full civic and social equality in the modern state; and the other for assimilation, as manifested in all the great activity, both individual and communal, in this period which was aimed at reducing the specifically Jewish content of Jewish life, and at bringing about the greatest possible merging of the Jews with the peoples in whose midst they dwelt and deepening their sense of national, social and spiritual identity with them.[10] But the first in time and importance of these two movements was the one for emancipation which determined the whole spiritual development of Jewry in these years. Assimilation was only, so to speak, a social and cultural reflection of emancipation; and the nationalist awakening came in a period of political reaction, when the Jews banded together in self-defense. The struggle between emancipation and reaction is thus paralleled by the struggle between assimilation and nationalism; and these two conflicts in fact constitute the whole content of modern Jewish history. It is therefore the historical course of the movement for emancipation that determines the different phases of Jewish history in modern times.

II

However, the prevailing view of more recent scholarship is that the beginning of the "modern period" in Jewish history should be pushed back much further.[11] The arguments for this earlier dating are clear enough. For, even if it is agreed that Enlightenment and Emancipation were the two most important and significant phenomena in the life of modern Jewry, it will still not be correct to identify the beginning of the *Haskalah* with the work of Mendelssohn, and the beginning of the Emancipation with the

French Revolution. It is true, of course, that the *Haskalah* movement aimed at making the Jews of the day aware of the need for a purely rationalistic reappraisal of historical realities, and even attempted such a reappraisal of its own, on the basis of which it advocated that Jewish life and education should be brought into line with the requirements of reason and the demands of the time. It is also true that the *Haskalah* sought to reform educational methods and to improve public and domestic conduct, challenged the absolute spiritual authority of religious tradition, and even went so far as to pour scorn on time-honored customs and to repudiate accepted beliefs. Nevertheless, from the historical standpoint, it is not true that these revolutionary changes in Jewish life were brought about by the searching criticism of the *Haskalah*. Indeed, the exact opposite is the case: it was only after the foundations of traditional Jewish life had already been shaken that they also began to be subjected to rationalistic criticism. It was the collapse of the whole structure of Jewish beliefs and values that led to the individual Jew's self-effacement vis-à-vis the gentile world, thus leaving that whole generation of Jews all too ready to be influenced by the cultures of the nations amongst whom they lived, to steep themselves in their opinions and outlooks, and to adopt their manners and ways of life. It was only after this new feeling of life had penetrated into certain circles of the upper strata of Jewish society, and only after the elements of this different outlook on the world had taken root in their hearts, that another attitude to the religious tradition and the accepted Jewish way of life made itself felt. Then it was that the *Haskalah* also appeared on the scene as a social movement whose watchword was rationalistic criticism. The aim of this criticism was thus to rebuild a world that was already in the process of being destroyed. It is therefore historically correct to date the beginnings of the *Haskalah* movement back to the processes which led to the collapse of the inner world of Judaism. The origins of these processes are rooted in the failure of the Sabbatai Zevi movement, and their most striking symptoms had, by the first half of the eighteenth century, become part of the normal phenomena of Jewish life.[12]

The same is true of Jewish Emancipation. This is not to be regarded merely as a matter of political proclamation, or juridical principle, or civil courtesy. Like the movement for Jewish Enlightenment, Emancipation also comprises the whole complex of the processes by which the Jews became an organic part of the economic, civic, cultural and political fabric of the nations among whom they lived and the states in which they dwelt. And the origins of these processes, as has been conclusively proved by the most recent historical research, go back ultimately to the vital functions performed by the Jews in organizing the economies of the modern nation-states, functions which in fact had already become part of the normal features of Jewish life by the first half of the eighteenth century. Not a few able and enterprising Jews rose to positions of power and amassed great wealth. The secular rulers needed them for their experience and advice, their practical efficiency and organizational talent. Whether these Jews were purveyors of military supplies or procurors of loans, minters of coins or financial agents, jewel merchants or "court" speculators, traders or industrialists—or practised all these occupations simultaneously—they were in every case always firmly entrenched in the secular life of the state.[13] The great majority of them, it is true, contented themselves with the economic power and royal favor that they enjoyed, and frequently sought to demonstrate their aloofness from political affairs. But, even so, the economic position occupied in the state by this upper stratum of the Jewish community was an augury for the future, the first step in the full integration of the Jews into the life of their host nations. Moreover, the fate of these few "great Jews" was itself of very great general historical significance. Take, for example, the well-known case of Züss Oppenheimer, the financial agent of the Duke of Würtemberg, who rose from being a subordinate tax-farmer to the position of chief political advisor, and even tried to draw conclusions from this meteoric rise with regard to his own way of life and his conduct in non-Jewish society, only to end his days on the gallows. His life-story not only illustrates the actual nature of the "integration" of this stratum of "great Jews" into the fabric of the secular state, but also brings out the tension of the struggle which, already in those early days, was inseparable from this process. Much the same lesson may also be learned from the story, a few decades earlier, of the checkered career of Samuel Oppenheimer in Vienna.

This rise of the upper stratum of the Jewish community marks the beginning of "modern times" in Jewish history, since it provided the social framework both for the growth of the *Haskalah* movement and for the first stirrings in Jewry of the struggle for emancipation.

III

There are also other reasons for putting back the beginning of the modern period in Jewish history to the first part of the eighteenth century. "Enlightenment" and "emancipation" are far from exhausting the whole content of the historical reality of Jewish life in modern times, even if we use these terms in their widest possible sense and attribute to the power and influence of these two movements both the radical change in the professional composition of Jewry that occurred in these generations, and also the social, cultural and political awakening of the Jewish masses and their emergence as an active new factor in determining the nation's destiny in this period. A historiographical approach which regards the enlightenment and the emancipation as the central features of modern Jewish history entirely fails to take account of, or at least relegates into the background, some of the most important aspects of Jewish life in modern times, those very aspects in which the "historical activity" of Jewry in those times was in fact most intensely displayed. The rise of the great new centers of Jewish population which came into being in this period in Russia, North America and Palestine, where, in a short span of years, masses of Jews were concentrated in unprecedented numbers; the origin, growth and spread of *Hassidism* which, in the mass-appeal of its religious revivalism, the persistence of its influence and the effectiveness of its organization, had for generations had no parallel in Jewish history;[14] the movement of "revolt against the *Galut* (Exile)" which, during the last sixty years, has gradually and steadily spread to all sections of the Jewish people, renewing its political and cultural unity, and rousing it to acts and achievements such as had not been performed by Jews since the beginning of the Dispersion, and which changed the whole character of the nation—all these vital developments do not, according to

86

the accepted historiographical viewpoint, constitute the framework of modern Jewish history; indeed, they are not even in the mainstream, so to speak, of this period and can only be brought into it by the *Haskalah* and Emancipation movements.

Such a historical point of view is obviously untenable. The beginning of the modern period in Jewish history cannot be fixed without due attention being paid to the first halting-places in the mass migration of Jews which had already started from the centers of Jewish population in eastern Europe and the countries of Islam in the early part of the eighteenth century, with the first clear indications of the approaching decline and extinction of those centers. Nor can the limits of this period be determined without proper note being taken of the beginnings of *Hassidism*, which developed out of the inner disintegration of the communal structure of Polish Jewry as a result of the crisis through which the latter passed in the first part of the same century. And account must also be taken of the appearance at this time of the first proponents of the revolt against the *Galut*, orthodox Messianists who, undaunted by the failure of messianic mysticism, persevered determinedly in their search for new ways of bringing nearer the redemption and finding an outlet for their pent-up messianic energies.

IV

Also from the standpoint of the official attitude to the Jews and their civic status, the beginning of the eighteenth century is marked by several phenomena which are to be regarded as indicative of the modern period. The English philosopher and freethinker who advocated religious toleration and full civil rights for the Jews, and who attributed the decline of Spain to its expulsion of the Jews and the rise of Holland, in part, to that country's tolerant attitude to its Jewish citizens, was far from being an exception in his day.[15] Even Sicilian monks pointed to the wealth of Leghorn as proof of the blessings brought to that flourishing city by its Jewish community, and expressed the hope that Jews would come to settle in their midst too, bringing economic prosperity with them.[16] The widespread growth of the interest shown by Christian theological circles, at the beginning of the eighteenth century, in rabbinical literature, in Jewish religious customs and practices, and in Judaism's attitude to Christianity, was also connected, to no small degree, with the first gentile realization of the new position now occupied by the Jews in the life of their countries of residence, and the consequent need for a revision of age-old prejudices.

The Dutch scholar who translated the *Mishnah* into Latin, and was even inclined to admit the sanctity of the Jewish Oral Law, sought to give added weight to his demand that greater attention be paid by Christians to rabbinical literature by stressing the importance of the principle of toleration followed by the Free Republic of Holland with regard to the Jews, and also the gratitude felt by Jews to the state that had granted them full civic rights.[17] Even in a "History of the Jews" written at the beginning of the eighteenth century by an orthodox Christian from the bigoted theological conception of the Jews as a people "abandoned by God" and permeated with anti-

Jewish religious polemic, it is evident that the author was drawn to the subject by his recognition of the Jewish nation's indestructibility. His interest in the spirit that had kept Judaism alive through two thousand years of persecution was aroused by the changes in Jewish status which were occurring before his own eyes and which showed him and his contemporaries that the Jewish people was far from extinct, despite all the trials and tribulations through which it had passed.[18]

Indeed, even such a warped and viciously anti-Semitic scholar as Eisenmenger was affected by the modern atmosphere of his time. Having collected together all the old ignorant and stupid lies and poisonous libels ever uttered about the Jews and Judaism, he tried to bring them up to date by interlarding the whole farrago of hatred with such "modern" themes as the economic rise of the Jews and the civic rights enjoyed by Amsterdam Jewry who, in their new-found freedom, even presumed to make strongly critical remarks about Christianity and to advocate openly the truth of their own opinions and beliefs.[19] The subsequent fate of Eisenmenger's book—the attempt, at first successful, made by the Jewish communal leaders and by influential individual Jews to have the publication of the book banned as a threat to the public peace—is also indicative of the arrival of the modern era in Jewish history: the secular governments now consider themselves obliged to include the Jews too in their concern for the preservation of the public peace—under pressure, of course, from the Jews themselves to whose appeals they cannot, on account of the latter's economic position, remain indifferent.[20]

89

V

Modern Jewish history begins with the immigration to Palestine of one thousand Jews led by Rabbi Judah the Pious in the year 1700. The great significance of this act for the vital content of Jewish history in those times does not lie only in the symbolical value of this organized mass immigration to the Holy Land under the leadership of a prophet of redemption, himself a religious rebel against the *Galut*, as a portent for the future, a pointer to generations whose historical experience was largely one of mass revolts and mass migrations in search of national salvation. Of no less importance were the causes of this immigration, the way in which it was organized, and the nature and consequences of its failure, all of them signs of the twilight of the Middle Ages and the dawn of the modern era.

Following as it did on the decline of the Sabbatai Zevi movement, this immigration not only demonstrated the persistence of the messianic ferment and the continuity of "the boundless yearning"[21] to hasten the redemption in every possible way; it also marked the beginning of a more realistic course of messianic activity which made it possible to keep alive the eagerness for redemption in the common people's hearts by finding for it forms of expression that could be unquestionably accepted into the fabric of Jewish life. The immigration of pious, God-fearing and observant Jews, and the resettlement of the Land of Israel by their labors, now came to be regarded as a necessary preliminary to the redemption of the whole nation. The immigration of this first organized group prepared the way for all the waves of immigration that followed during the next hundred and seventy years. Immigration to Palestine, by separate individuals and whole groups, henceforward became a very common phenomenon. Particularly numerous amongst the immigrants were great Sages of the Law and famed Cabbalists, many from the important congregations of the Western Diaspora, but some also from the remote and isolated Oriental communities. Their total number ran into hundreds.[22] From their ranks subsequently came those emissaries from the Land of Israel who worked to spread a greater awareness of the importance of the *Yishuv* for the whole of Jewry and its vital role in hastening the redemption, and thereby to increase the influence of the *Yishuv* and strengthen its spiritual authority over the communities of the Diaspora.[23]

Every one of these groups of immigrants had to pass through a period of great hardship in establishing itself in the country; and at the same time, the resulting growth in the population of the *Yishuv* still further increased its economic difficulties and made it urgently necessary to organize the financial assistance provided by the Diaspora communities on an efficient and permanent basis (the *Halukah*). The result of this dual effort was the steady growth of the old *Yishuv*—the Jewish population dwelling within the walls of the "four towns" (Jerusalem, Hebron, Safed, and Tiberias)—which in modern times exercised a kind of magnetic attraction over all those men of vision who refused to bow to the prevailing trends and could not come to terms with the new spirit of nihilism and atheism which was sweeping through the whole world, and from which Judaism too was not exempt. By its devoted preservation of this special character, the old *Yishuv* became a new and very influential factor in the strengthening of the physical bonds between the nation and its land, to an extent unequalled for many generations. However, this extreme conservatism of the old *Yishuv* was not the sole characteristic of the early groups of religious immigrants, any more than asceticism was the only dominant trend amongst them.[24] There were also other elements and other sects, including even "the Sabbatians," heretical followers of Sabbatai Zevi who regarded the abolition of all religious prohibitions and restrictions as the first step towards bringing about the nation's redemption. These other circles also had no small influence at first, even in Jerusalem, though they were not able to maintain themselves there for long and most of them eventually left the country, while some even adopted Islam.[25] Nevertheless, when these emigrants returned to Europe they created a considerable stir there. Only a few of them abandoned Judaism and cut themselves off from their people completely. Of the remaining majority, some joined the underground followers of Sabbatai Zevi and helped to direct their propaganda, thus reinforcing the active opposition in the various congregations to the established religious and social leadership;[26] while others, by encouraging the spread of a laxer approach to the observance of the practical commandments, still further increased the disregard of the rabbinical authorities already prevalent in wide circles of Jewry. Both these developments formed an integral and important part of the whole spiritual environment which gave rise to the *Haskalah* movement as the dominant force in Jewish life in the Diaspora. The symbolic significance of the immigration to Palestine of Rabbi Judah the Pious and his group of followers as marking the beginning of modern Jewish history is thus not merely historical and ideological, but must be considered, both in conception and execution, in its social and physical aspects too. Seen from this standpoint, it was an ideological and social expression of the *Wanderlust* which had already gripped considerable sections of east European Jewry who, feeling their whole existence as Jews threatened, especially in Poland, by a growing sense of territorial and physical insecurity and fear of the morrow, began a mass migration to the countries of central and western Europe, entering these lands and filtering into their Jewish communities, despite all the legal and physical obstacles placed in their way.[27] Hence, Rabbi Judah's immigration to Palestine also symbolically marks the beginning of the migratory movement of Jews which is to be regarded as one of the most distinctive characteristics of Jewish history in modern times.

There was also something entirely new in the fact that this was an *organized* immigration; and both the nature and the purpose of its organization also mark the opening of the modern era in Jewish history. Neither the existing Jewish congregation nor the authorized institutions of Jewry played any part in the planning and execution of the whole enterprise, which was carried out entirely by a new grouping of social elements brought into being by a common ideology. This is the first full-scale instance of the unifying, dynamic force of "ideology" which was to play such an important part in the whole course of modern Jewish history, from the first bands of *Hassidim* down to the organized political parties of our own day. This first organized group of immigrants did not fall apart on its arrival in Palestine, but remained knit together and formed a new community or congregation, a new social unit, which was headed not by rabbis or communal lead-

ers, but by *Hassidim*, men whose authority was derived
from the power of their own personality and was never a
matter for dispute. The immigration of the group was
made possible by the help that it received from various
Diaspora communities and from wealthy and influential
individuals in them, and also by the great moral support
given it by the Jewish masses. This popular sympathy was
due both to the personal influence of the "leader" (Rabbi
Judah the Pious) and to the opposition to official Jewry
implicit in the whole enterprise. Here is the prototype of
the hassidic "congregation of the pious" and "community
of the righteous" which Rabbi Judah's group closely re-
sembled not only in name, but also in form of organization. A further feature of this *aliyah* which is of symbolic
significance for the modern era in Jewish history is its
"pan-Jewishness." The original members of the group,
who came from Poland, were joined by immigrants from
Germany, Hungary and Moravia, and assistance was
provided by many congregations in Germany, Austria,
Holland and Turkey.[28]

No other event of that time was destined to have such a
deep and lasting effect on all the different paths subsequently followed by Jewish history in modern times as
this immigration, the starting-point of the many and varied highways and byways that have led to the heights and
depths, the glories and tragedies of this decisive, turbulent
and tortured period. It therefore seems to me only right
that the modern epoch, which ends with the international
recognition of the independent Jewish State of Israel
following upon the holocaust of European Jewry, should
begin with this first large, organized group of immigrants
who believed that, by saving themselves from the impend-

ing catastrophe of European Jewry, they were heralding the Redemption.

VI

Tremendous changes occurred, in the modern era, in all the lands where Jews lived, changes which not only affected the political regimes and administrative structures of the states in question as well as the civic status and cultural level of their peoples, but also revolutionized their whole social and economic order. In many of these countries there were also numerous changes in the ethnic composition of the population. Although these transformations usually resulted from factors entirely outside the sphere of Jewish history, they nevertheless created for the Jews living in these countries conditions of life completely different from those in previous generations. This development as such was nothing new in Jewish history; indeed, it was simply a repetition of what happened in every period of the nation's life in the Diaspora. The historical activity of the Jews was always confined within the bounds of a certain general historical framework, within which alone the Jews in every period could continue to lead their specifically Jewish existence—founding communities, organizing congregations and creating their own way of life. But the scope and character of the above mentioned changes that occurred in modern times so blurred the outline of collective Jewish existence and so reduced the inner content of Judaism, that it becomes necessary first to determine the limits of specifically Jewish history in this period. Although the reduction of the inner content of Judaism is undoubtedly connected with the decline of the Jewish religion as a formative factor in the life of the nation, it is not to be regarded as merely the result of this decline. The uniqueness of Judaism throughout history has lain in its being a self-contained, distinctive way of life embracing the whole existence both of the individual Jew and of the entire community. There is, of course, no doubt that this Jewish way of life was based on the Law, and that the Law—in the sense of a set of beliefs and opinions, views and ideas—was always and at all times the living soul of the practical observances of Judaism. It is equally clear, however, that this way of life could never have come into being without the previous existence of the Jews as a corporate body, without their collective will to live together, and without the possibility thus afforded them of creating their own pattern of life even on foreign soil. Now, it is precisely in modern times that this Jewish "corporateness" has been most seriously impaired. First of all, the power of the secular state and its influence in moulding the lives of all its citizens has greatly increased. Many aspects of life that had previously come within the jurisdiction of the religious community or the local congregation, of the class corporation or the trade guild, of the family or the individual, were now brought—directly or indirectly—under state control. The organizational barriers which had existed between the individual and the state were now for the most part removed, and such few as still remained had no more effective force. The jurisdiction of the organized Jewish community was steadily reduced until in theory, and often in practice too, it was finally limited to synagogal affairs and to matters directly connected with divine worship, in the narrowest sense of the term. And even here the state frequently made its authority strongly felt, in pursuance of its aim of bringing all the activities of its citizens under its supervision. In the end, the state's authority became so firmly established, and its power and efficiency so strong, that it was no longer content with its citizens' performance of their civic duties, but demanded the possession of their hearts, spirits and souls.

This contraction of the specifically Jewish content of Jewish life had already been keenly felt in the first generation after the achievement of Emancipation, and even in the thick of the struggle for it. The Jews of that time accepted this development as inevitable, since they thought that their very existence in the modern state depended on their being equal to the gentiles in everything. The state could either recognize them as full citizens and grant them full civic rights, or it could place them entirely outside the modern society that was then taking shape and make them bear all the consequences of this exclusion.[29] To remain inside modern society on the former basis was impossible. The Jews therefore accepted state interference in their own affairs, because they clearly understood that they could not both fight for their right to be recognized by the state as its citizens, and at the same time demand that the state's authority be restricted where they were concerned.

As the power and authority of the state increased, so the influence of the "corporate" element in Judaism declined. The individual Jew was set free from the jurisdiction of the Jewish community, in part by his own conscious will and effort. The economic integration of the Jews into the life of the state was accompanied by a process of cultural assimilation. In his daily life the Jew became more and more a part of the environment in which he had made his home and in which he lived and worked. The new social conditions enabled him to take an active and effective part in politics and public affairs. An outlet was thus provided for his energies outside the Jewish community, and his activity in these fields integrated him still more fully into the social, cultural, civic and political milieu of the nation in whose midst he dwelt.

Such activities on the part of individual Jews, however, do not come, and cannot be brought, within the purview of Jewish history, despite the large numbers of the Jews involved. They belong rather to the history of the gentile nation or community in which these Jews did their work. Moreover, as the Jews participated more and more actively in the social life of the peoples in whose midst they dwelt and integrated themselves more and more thoroughly into their cultures, so the mutual estrangement of the various different Jewish communities increased. Even the keen awareness of the "oneness" of the Jewish nation, which had been so vitally important throughout all the centuries of the Diaspora, steadily evaporated in modern times. The uniform Jewish way of life, which had once given every Jew the feeling of being "at home" in a Jewish house in any and every place in the world, was also very seriously affected,[30] so much so that in some countries there remained of it only a few pathetic relics, memorials as it were of a vanished world. The cultural cooperation between the Jewish communities seemed to have come to an end. Even in matters of Jewish law and Jewish religion there was no longer any mutual understanding, not even in official rabbinical circles. But what apparently suffered

98

most was the sense of sharing a common destiny. A leading German Jew of the nineteenth century could, at the time of the Damascus blood libel, say that the fate of the whole of Oriental Jewry was for him less important than the licence to open a pharmacy that was to be given to a Jew in Prussia.[31] Hebrew, which had first been the cultural instrument employed by the united nation in creating its religious law and pattern of life, and later the living language of the common historical destiny that bound together the separate parts of the nation in dispersion, no longer performed its functions in most of the Jewish communities.[32] The language declined as its functions disappeared. This decline of Hebrew was a striking indication of the extinction of Jewish unity in the lands of the Diaspora. Nor is it correct to ascribe these phenomena only to certain periods of the modern era, periods of assimilation, repudiation of Jewishness, and the like. The truth is that they belong to the permanent historical pattern of recent generations. In the days of the *Hibbat Zion* movement and the great national awakening, at the time when Ahad Ha-am was issuing his call for "spiritual preparation" of the Jewish masses, hundreds of new Jewish primary schools were opened in Russia, through both private and communal initiative and with the aid of public funds; and in these schools tens upon tens of thousands of Jewish children were educated entirely in the Russian language and on Russian literature, to the total neglect of Hebrew studies.[33] Yet, at the same time, throughout this period we can also feel the continued existence of Jewry as an indissoluble entity. During all these generations Jewish life was carried on with a vigorous, restless intensity and the Jewish struggle for survival also continued unabated. Even the active participation of Jews in the social, political, cultural and spiritual lives of the countries in which there was a considerable Jewish population sometimes appears to be a distinctive historical trend which derives its special character from the life force of Jewish uniqueness. The limits of specifically Jewish history in modern times are thus not chronological, but social, and are to be defined in terms of developments in the following fields: the attempt to "break through" on to the stage of world events, accompanied by a stubborn struggle to preserve a distinctive, centuries-old spiritual and social entity; the emergence of a new pattern of Jewish life, resulting from a constant process of adaptation to the non-Jewish environment, side by side with a constant renewal of Jewish uniqueness; and the crystallization of certain tendencies in the collective will of the Jewish people, arising from their ideological unification and their organization for national self-defense.

VII

The basic premise for the understanding of Jewish history is the continued unity of the Jewish nation even in dispersion. This means that, through the period of the Diaspora and right down to modern times (when Jewish communities had spread almost everywhere over the habitable surface of the globe), the Jewish people constituted a distinctive national entity, the different parts of which were linked together in a common destiny by certain unique life processes peculiar to them alone. Even though the social, political, cultural and economic changes that occurred in modern times made great inroads into the distinctively Jewish way of life and drastically reduced the "sense of entirety" of world Jewry, the Jews nevertheless continued to belong to this entity and to live their lives as parts of it; nor did the gentile world ever cease to be conscious of its separate existence.

A proper appreciation of this "Jewish entity" is a prerequisite for the understanding of modern Jewish history. The reason for this is plain. The general historical changes which caused such a great revolution in Jewish life did not come about in a vacuum, but took place inside a certain clearly defined political and social entity with its own distinctive traditional forms. However, although the general direction taken by these changes was thus dependent on developments outside the specifically Jewish sphere, their impact on Jewish life was in no small measure determined both by the stability of Jewry and also by its adaptability to its environment. This is how there came about that "breakthrough" on to the stage of world history, as a result of which Jewish life underwent a great transformation, yet still remained essentially Jewish, though in a new guise. A discussion of the character and permanence of the uniform "Jewish entity" at the beginning of the modern era is thus one of the important preliminaries for the proper understanding of modern Jewish history.

The rapidity and extent of the transformations that have occurred in modern Jewish history seem sometimes to have made historians forget the fundamental axiom that, just as motion can only be apprehended in relation to rest, so the dynamic impetus of historical changes cannot be correctly understood unless proper attention is also paid to the static forces which tend to the preservation of the previously existing situation. In this connection, it must not be forgotten that Judaism is a historical phenomenon of great antiquity. The Jews are a very old historical nation with strong traditions which permeate their everyday life and are deeply embedded in their national consciousness. The existence of a specific Jewish entity is recognized both by the Jews themselves and by the outside world. This distinctive entity of Jewry was molded, in the course of many generations, by the national destiny of the Jews and their religious uniqueness, combined with their peculiar cultural and social character. Many and various were the conditions and circumstances which brought this entity into being—from the conquest of territories and the settlement of desert places, from national freedom and political independence to the harshness of bondage and the bitterness of exile, to dispersion amongst the nations and adaptation to a foreign environment. The national destiny of the Jews was forged on the long road followed by the nation in its transformations from "the children of Israel" into "the people of Israel," from "the community of Israel" into "the congregation of Israel," and from "the house of Israel" into "the remnant of Israel." And it was this journey that made Israel at once the oldest and one of the youngest nations in the world. The unique character of the Jewish religion—with its combination of philosophical doctrine, practical code of individual and communal life, and cabbalistic mysticism —was constantly at work throughout all this long period, creating ways of life and patterns of consciousness that were shared alike by all the parts of the dispersed nation. Indeed, Jewish self-awareness and self-examination have always been an inseparable part of Jewish history. The Jewish way of life has always been in some way involved in the mainstream of general history. Even the self-awareness of the ancient Israelites as "a people dwelling alone, and not reckoning itself among the nations"[34] resulted from their first clash with the outside world. From those early days onward a ceaseless struggle has been waged between two conflicting tendencies within the nation—the one to wholesale assimilation and the other to self-preservation—from Isaiah's castigation of the influence of ancient "wisdom" in Israel ("they are full of foreign customs") and the prohibition of the study of "Greek learning" during the cultural ascendency of Hellenism, to the polemics that raged around the works of Maimonides and the study of philosophy and the sciences, and to the historical criticism in the time of the Renaissance. The formation of the nation's cultural character is connected with this age-long struggle which had a powerful influence on the spiritual life of Jewry in every period—on the upbringing of its children and the education of its youth, on its intellectual level and ways of thought—and profoundly affected all the categories of Hebrew literature. Through this struggle, the foreign languages spoken by the Jews were, so to speak, "Judaized" by being emptied of their non-Jewish content and even given a flavor of sanctity; while the Hebrew language, which held the scattered Jewish communities together through the long generations of the Dispersion, became the instrument through which different cultures met and blended. It was this struggle, in which, openly or secretly, consciously or unconsciously, every single member of the nation was deeply involved, that fashioned the type of the educated and cultured Jew, giving him his distinctively Jewish characteristics of tense intellectual alertness, quick intuition of coming changes, and deep emotional concern for the fate of his disappearing ancient heritage.

The Jews also had a very well-formed, distinctive social

character all of their own. Even many generations after the destruction of Jerusalem and the loss of Jewish independence, the historical and social experience of those early times continued to exercise an influence over Jewish life. Memories of the past and the "lessons" of those far off days were still a living reality and still constituted the foundations of Jewish education and social training. The traditional veneration for the deeds of the patriarchs and the rule of the Judges, for the verdicts handed down by Kings and the rebukes uttered by Prophets, for the spiritual leadership of Priests and political supremacy of Princes was continued, generation after generation, in the respectful regard shown by the nation for the patriarchate of its sages and the integrity of its magistrates, for the righteousness of its administrators,[35] and the rule of its civic leaders, as well as for the greatness and wisdom of its rabbis. But the principal factor in the formation of the distinctive social character of the Jewish nation during its dispersion was its organization in separate holy congregations throughout the Diaspora. These congregations owed their origin and character to a combination of two elements— the one, collective self-defense, arising from the necessity to provide some protection against the dangers to which Jewish life was constantly exposed; and the other, collective acceptance of "the yoke of the kingdom of heaven," resulting from a willing readiness to join forces in promoting the worship of God, the observance of His commandments, and the study of His Law. These two elements united to form the peculiarly Jewish way of life, permeated by the warm intimacy of the home and family, but also subject to the rigorous supervision of spiritual guides and communal leaders charged with upholding the divine laws and enforcing the practical commandments, whose authority was imposed and accepted with the iron discipline demanded of the inhabitants of a beleaguered city. The very character of such a regime endowed it with a powerful religious sanction, while at the same time giving every individual the right and the power to call its authority in question on genuinely religious grounds. Hence, every objection developed, by the nature of things, into a kind of domestic quarrel, every criticism became a revolt against divine authority, and every act of opposition was, at its highest, a struggle for sacred principles and, at its lowest, a kind of civil war. These basic features of Judaism were common to all the members of the nation wherever they might be. Together they combined to create something which can be called "a Jewish climate," the special spiritual and social atmosphere whose air was breathed by every Jew everywhere. Across this special atmosphere radiated the waves of mutual influence between the various communities of the Diaspora, and through it passed the channels of their reciprocal social and psychological impulses. It also constituted the historical setting for the continued unity of the nation even in dispersion. This historical "field" was also conditioned by the beliefs about the Jews traditionally held by the gentile nations with whose religious, cultural, and sometimes even historical, heritage the Jewish past was so closely interwoven. This "Jewish tradition" of the gentiles was more than a mere recognition of the historical continuity of Judaism and its unique national and religious character; it was also a traditional attitude to the Jews, an attitude made up of prejudices and religious bigotry, of xenophobia and jealous rivalry, of habitual contempt and profound mistrust. This

105

was especially the case in times of upheaval and confusion, when the Jews served as scapegoats for the misdeeds of the non-Jewish populace and its leaders, and it was expedient—and sometimes even necessary—to revive the "old tradition" of Jew-hatred as an effective and well-proven means of justifying new anti-Jewish measures. This constantly renewed tradition of hatred inevitably evoked in the Jewish communities repercussions and reactions which were also, by the nature of the case, of a uniform character.[36] The traditional gentile attitude to the Jews thus deepened the Jews' sense of sharing a common fate, maintained the tension of their Jewishness at a uniform level, and helped to bind together the communities of the Diaspora in a living unity.

Now, there are no solid grounds, it seems to me, for doubting the existence of this Jewish unity in modern times too. The far-flung dispersion of the Jews over all the countries of the world and their division into separate units living amongst different peoples, their integration into the economic, cultural and social fabric of the lives of these peoples, the barriers of various kinds erected between one Jewish community and another—all these were circumstances that greatly hampered and weakened this Jewish unity and modified its character, but they did not affect its actual existence. It continued in being, both as a living reality and as a framework for the "Jewish tension" shared alike by all the communities, these being the two different facets of that special "Jewish climate" which has always been the uniform setting of Jewish history. It is undoubtedly true, of course, that the Jews in modern times were right at the center of the processes leading to the civic and cultural unity of the peoples in whose midst they re-

106

sided, that they played a part—sometimes a considerable one—in the political consolidation of their nationalist states, and that they actively participated both in the economic progress and unification of these countries and in the development of their democratic regimes. The signs of this active Jewish participation in the national and political coalescence of the gentile nations were clearly discernible in all the various spheres of public life: in journalism and literature, in art and science, in political debates and social movements, at party conferences and at parliamentary sessions, in commerce and industry, and in schools and institutes of learning. Moreover, all these processes of emergent nationhood evoked an unmistakable and powerful response within the Jewish community: considerable sections of the Jewish population now completely identified themselves, in spirit, with the nationalism of the peoples in whose midst they lived and worked.[37] This being so, it is not surprising that objections have very frequently been raised by scholars to the conception of the unity of the dispersed Jewish nation in modern times as a fact of dynamic importance. However, it must not be forgotten that the same processes of unification and consolidation which were at work in the lives of other peoples also had their effect on Jewish life. While keeping the communities of the Diaspora apart in some ways, they also brought them together in others. Just as modern means of communication and economic cooperation broke down the barriers separating the different regions of every country, so these same circumstances also made it easier for the Jews of the Diaspora to get to know each other at close quarters and reduced the distances and the mutual ignorance which had previously kept them apart. In the same way as the traditional divisions between different ethnic groups in the same nation were removed by the introduction of a uniform system of popular education and the teaching of the nation's past as an important factor in the training of the young, so the self-knowledge of the Jews and their sense of sharing a common destiny were increased by the *Haskalah* movement—however small its scope—and by the development of the "Science of Judaism" and of Jewish literature in Hebrew and other languages. The popular press awakened the interest of the gentile lower classes in social, national and political affairs, and the democratic regime aroused them to political activity and developed their awareness of their national responsibility. In the same way the Jewish press —not only in Hebrew and Yiddish, but in all languages— carried information about the situation of Jews throughout the world to every corner of the Diaspora, and thus stimulated the interest taken in their lives and fortunes;[38] while the participation of the non-Jewish masses in social and political affairs galvanized the Jewish masses into playing an active part in Jewish life. In these and similar ways the processes listed here helped in the creation of that "Jewish climate" which, in modern times no less than in previous ages, has been the basis of the unity of the Jewish nation. The nature of that unity can be best explained and illustrated by a few historical examples.

First, the waves of Jewish migration in modern times. These scattered the Jewish population and depleted the centers of Jewish settlement, severing age-long communal ties and snapping family and domestic bonds. The solid mass of Jewry was splintered into fragments and the individual Jewish emigrant was cast into the melting-pot of new countries in which he was a complete stranger, where there was no Jewish tradition and he could do whatever he pleased. In these lands he therefore shook off a great deal of that way of life which had previously been an integral part of his Jewishness.

However, this picture, though correct as far as it goes, is not the whole historical truth, since it omits the positive content of the migratory process when seen in its entirety. The mass migration of millions of Jews, the great majority of whom were devoid of all means of subsistence and had no civic rights in the countries which they left and through which they passed, and their settlement in new lands whose languages and customs they did not know and their rapid integration into the life of those countries—all this was an achievement beyond the powers of the individual initiative of each separate emigrant. Seen from the historical standpoint, it was a national enterprise of vast proportions made possible by concentrated, sustained efforts on the part of the primary cells in the Jewish social organism: the close-knit unity of the Jewish family; the fraternal ties which, in the foreign land, bound together those who had come from the same community; and the constant assistance given by the organized Jewish public, whether in the old traditional Jewish manner by means of charitable societies and voluntary contributions, or in more sophisticated modern fashion through emigration committees, settlement societies, associations of people from the same locality (*Landsmannschaften*), associations for mutual aid, and the like—all these being a concrete and direct expression of the sense of a common Jewish destiny and of mutual Jewish responsibility. All this sustained and intense activity, this ceaseless tapping of the forces latent in the nation, so far from weakening these primary cells of the social organism of Jewry, actually increased their vitality.

The waves of emigration knit the Jewish family still closer together, strengthened still further the fraternal ties uniting all the former members of the same community in their new land, and at the same time created the new forms that were essential for the organization of world Jewry on modern lines. They furthermore brought the Jews of different countries into actual physical contact with each other. The routes followed by the emigrants were like so many bridges spanning the distances separating the different communities of the Diaspora, across which the traffic flowed in a ceaseless stream and in various directions throughout the modern period, from the eighteenth century onward. The main movement was from east to west: from Poland, Lithuania and Russia to Germany and the lands of western Europe, and above all to the United States;[39] from Italy to England, and so forth.[40] But there were also other directions: the Jews of Lithuania and White Russia emigrated to the Ukraine, to the interior of Russia beyond the Pale of Settlement; the Jews of the Ukraine, to Galicia and Romania; the Jews of Galicia to Hungary; the Jews of European Turkey to Hungary and France; the Jews of North Africa to France and Italy;[41] and there was also even a migration from Germany and Russia to Poland,[42] and from Austria to the interior of Russia.

All this was in addition to the constant movement of Jews within each state, from one district to another, from villages and "settlements" to country towns, and from country towns to large cities. For generations the Jews' freedom of movement had been restricted and they had been permitted to reside only in certain specifically stated areas. When these restrictions and prohibitions were abolished, the Jews exploited their new-found freedom of movement to the full. It was not only the Rothschild dynasty that had branches in Frankfurt and Paris, Vienna and London. Jewish families, all of whose members resided in one place, have been a rare phenomenon in Jewish life in modern times.

These mass migrations, as already stated, created a bridge between the different communities of the Diaspora and united them in a single spiritual climate. The upper stratum of Polish Jewry, especially in Warsaw, which in the nineteenth century played a very large role in the development of Polish industry, came in part from Germany[43] and was comprised of ardent assimilationists. And the first propagators of the *Haskalah* in Odessa were emigrants from Brody who played a large part in the development of Odessa's commerce and industry. Similarly, Hassidism was disseminated in Hungary by emigrants from Galicia,[44] and the proponents of the "Science of Judaism" in France were German Jewish scholars.[45]

A second illustration of Jewish unity is provided by one of the most important processes in modern Jewish history —the integration of the Jews into the economic life of the nations in which they lived. This process not only strengthened the connections of the Jews with the secular state and its rulers, but also brought them into closer contact with the non-Jewish population and its affairs. The Jews were actively engaged in the provision of military supplies; they played a large part in the organization of the state's economy, and in the efficient management of its export and import trade; and they devoted their wealth and strength to the development of its industry, by providing capital for new enterprises, finding markets for their products, and the like. Each one of these forms of economic activity, by bringing them into contact with a different sector of the gentile population and making them partners in the affairs and cares of the whole country, also resulted in closer social relations with non-Jews and a greater degree of cultural assimilation.

But in this case too it can be said that the above description, while correct in itself, does not do justice to the positive content of the process of economic and social integration seen as a whole. What we have here is, once again, not merely the success story of a number of outstanding Jews who rose to positions of power and fame thanks solely to their personal ability and talent. For here too the economic success of individual Jews was inseparable from the concerted efforts made, in accordance with their nature, by the primary cells of the Jewish social organism. Samuel Oppenheimer, for example, the fiscal agent of the Viennese court and the organizing genius who steered the Austrian economy through critical times, carried on his numerous and widely ramified financial deals with the help of scores of Jewish businessmen. These partners and sub-agents of his were scattered in more than fifty different localities,[46] not only on Austrian territory and in the German states, but in foreign countries too—in Holland and England, Italy and Turkey, Poland and Russia. The economic integration and social assimilation of the Jews of western Europe in the eighteenth century found ideological expression in the *Haskalah* movement and its ideals; and the Hebrew character of this movement, in its early stages, was bound up with a concerted

Jewish effort which led to the economic rise and social advancement of fairly large circles of western European Jewry.

A still more striking example of this kind is provided by the history of Russian Jewry in the nineteenth century. As is well known, the Jews of Russia played a very important part in the development of Russia's agricultural export trade with the countries of western Europe, in the attraction of western European capital to Russia and its use in the organization of the Russian banking system, and in the construction of Russia's railway system, the opening up of her mines, and the establishment of her heavy industry.[47] This cooperation between Jews and Russians formed the economic and social background of the ideology of "Russification" with which the *Haskalah* movement of the sixties and seventies of the last century was permeated. Here too the success of individual Jews in these fields was the result of a concerted Jewish effort. Not only were tens of thousands of other Jews actively involved in the economic integration of the few, but also the whole efficacy and success of this activity was, once again, conditioned by the character of the "primary cells" of the Jewish organism—by the close and intensive inter-Jewish cooperation in economic activity, by the degree of mutual trust existing between various Jewish communities and their joint organizational ability, by Russian Jewry's personal acquantanceship and close ties with wide circles of Jews in western Europe, and the like. As a result of these circumstances, the effort which the Jews put into this economic activity and the achivements which they gained thereby had a considerable influence on their new, growing national self-awareness and their increasing confidence in their own organizational and military ability. Thus, the *Hibbat Zion* movement, which arose among Russian Jewry at the beginning of the 1880's, was inspired by a great faith in the constructive powers and organizational talent of the Jews, the roots of which go back to the processes of economic integration in the sixties and seventies and the part played by the Jews in them.

The third example is taken from the cultural and political sphere. One of most distinctive features of the modern period in Jewish history is the social assimilation of the Jews—sometimes to the extent of their actual entry into gentile circles—and their active participation in the cultural life of the nations of Europe. This process, which began in the eighteenth century, gathered momentum in the nineteenth with the spread of democracy and the gradual freeing of social and cultural life from the exclusive control of the aristocracy, the bureaucracy and the Church. These circles, of course, did not relinquish this monopoly without a struggle. They were, by and large, bitter opponents of the new regime in Europe and its whole liberal spirit, using the full extent of their influence to resist every stage in its advance. They were greatly helped in this stubborn rearguard action by the European nations' weighty tradition of feudalism and ecclesiasticism and the all-pervading prevalence of the medieval spirit and outlook in their social culture, one of the elements of the latter being the tradition of Jew-baiting. Naturally enough these circles, so far from welcoming the entry of the Jews into Christian society, did everything they could to oppose it. Moreover, the immemorial tradition of hatred and contempt for the Jews made this anti-Semitism of the ruling classes an effective social and political weapon in their war

114

against the whole new order which aimed at raising to power all kinds of "upstarts" from the ranks of the under-privileged masses. In making their way into the social and cultural life of the gentile nations the Jews were on the defensive from the start. But the longer the struggle against the unyielding powers of reaction lasted and the fiercer it grew, the more pronounced did the apologetical and polemical note in their activity become. The Jews were compelled to stand up for their rights, frequently in a hostile atmosphere of prejudice and against a tradition of unfriendliness, if not worse.

In these historical circumstances they had no choice but to seek the fulfillment of their social and cultural ambitions through the new channels of the emergent democratic regime. Into this effort they had to pour all their intellectual and spiritual powers, all those distinctively Jewish characteristics which were the product of generations of life in the Diaspora and which had equipped them for a struggle of this kind. The age-long Jewish tradition of education and book learning had developed the intellectual acumen of the Jews and sharpened their debating powers; while the circumstances of their existence throughout the Diaspora period had trained them to be constantly on the alert and acutely sensitive to all the changes and fluctuations in the world around them. These and similar characteristics were also displayed, as they were obviously bound to be, in the literary, artistic, social and political forms taken by the integration of the Jews into the lives of the nations of Europe.

The non-Jews were keenly conscious of the distinctive quality of these Jewish national traits. Some of them, indeed, were generous, spirited and broad-minded enough to actually welcome the addition of a foreign element into their own culture. But the majority remained narrowly xenophobic and expressed bitter resentment, publicly or in private, against the "adulteration" of the nation's purity by the "Jewish spirit." At the same time, it can hardly be doubted that it was precisely these distinctively Jewish characteristics that won for the literary works and political activities of the Jewish assimilationists the sympathetic and admiring interest of their fellow Jews in other countries. Thus, the writer who exercised the greatest influence over the Russian Jewish intelligentsia in the sixties and seventies of the nineteenth century was Börne; and the poems of Heine found their way to the heart of every Jewish reader. Or there is the instructive case of David Gordon, a Lithuanian-born Jew who began his journalistic career in England and became assistant editor and subsequently editor of the first Hebrew newspaper *Hamaggid,* which, though published in Prussia, was read mainly in Russia and Poland. In his political articles in this paper, Gordon educated his numerous readers to adopt the liberal democratic outlook as demonstrated in the writings and activities of Jewish authors and politicians in the countries of central and western Europe. And the principal and most sincere mourners of the deaths of Eduard Lasker, the distinguished liberal German statesman,[48] and Gregory Gershoni, the dynamic Russian revolutionary, were the crowds of Jews who followed their remains to their last resting-places.

The actual character of this Jewish sense of unity, and the way in which this uniform "Jewish climate" was created in the modern period, are such important aspects of Jewish history in this period that it will, I think, be useful to give a few examples of the working of this unity at various times.

From the first half of the eighteenth century onward, M. H. Luzatto, the brilliantly precocious talmudic scholar, inspired cabbalist and gifted poet from Padua, the charm and power of whose personality deeply impressed all those around him, founded in his city a modest *yeshivah* "for the study of the Cabbalah, the restoration of the *Schehinah* and the regeneration of all Israel, the people of God." One of the "holy members" of this *yeshivah* was a young Lithuanian Jew (Gordon) from Vilna, a student of medicine at the University of Padua, who was so filled with admiration for his teacher that he descanted upon his greatness in a letter to Mordecai Yoffe-Schlesinger, one of the wealthy Jews of Vilna who was closely connected to many of the dignitaries of the Vilna community. Conversely, the later rabbinical opposition to Luzatto was not confined to the rabbis of Italy: indeed, the leading parts in it were played by R. Moses Ha-agiz, a native of Jerusalem and emissary from the Holy Land, who was then resident in Altona; by R. Jacob Cohen, the Chief Rabbi of Frankfurt, a native of Prague; and by R. Jacob Emden, who had been born in Altona and educated in Poland, had resided first in Moravia and then in Altona, and the members of whose family were to be found scattered in every Jewish community from London and Amsterdam to Brody in Galicia, Lissa in Greater Poland, and Old Konstantin in Volhynia. And when M. H. Luzatto stopped at Amsterdam on his way to settle in the Holy Land, he printed there his allegorical drama *Layesharim Tehillah* (*Praise to the Upright*), one of the works that had a very great influence on the new Hebrew poetry in Holland, Germany and Eastern

117

Europe, and also published his book *Mesillat Yesharim* (*A Path for the Righteous*) which became the classical text of the movement for moral reform (*Musar*) among the Jews of Lithuania.

Also, in the first half of that century, there was the great and popular Moroccan rabbi, Hayyim ben Atar. Passing through Italy on his way to settle in the Holy Land, this sage gathered round him there a band of disciples who joined him on his journey. Subsequently, he founded a *yeshivah* in Jerusalem; but his book *Or Hahayyim* (*The Light of Life*), which found its most admiring readers amongst the Ukrainian disciples and followers of the Baal Shem Tov, was published in Venice.

Next, an example from the second half of the eighteenth century—that of Moses Mendelssohn, a native of Dessau whose ancestors had come from Poland. As a young man Mendelssohn followed his teacher, Rabbi David Frankel, to Berlin to continue his religious studies with him. In Berlin, where his interest in the sciences and philosophy was first aroused, he came under the influence of a Polish Jewish scholar, Rabbi Israel of Zamose, a man with a profound grasp of philisophy and a keen understanding of mathematics who taught Gemara to the pupils of the religious school endowed by the wealthy communal leader, Feitel Ephraim, and who was renowned for his power of logical, perspicuous writing, and his patient and unassertive character. While Mendelssohn's general intellectual development came under this Polish Jew's guidance, he was taught languages by a young Jewish doctor from Prague (Kisch), and was introduced to the world of literature by a Berlin *Maskil* (Aaron Gomperz). The whole Mendelssohnian circle of *Maskilim* and its work for the furtherance of

118

Jewish Enlightenment—the translation of the Bible into German with a new commentary, and the founding of *Hameassef*, the first modern Hebrew periodical—were also the fruits of the combined endeavors of Jews from a variety of countries of origin—the German states, Poland and Lithuania, Holland and Italy. Moreover, their influence penetrated to every corner of the Jewish Diaspora—as far as Shiklov in White Russia and Alexandria in Egypt.

The same phenomenon can also be observed in the nineteenth century, even before the rise of the Zionist movement. Moses Sofer, a native of Frankfurt and pupil of its *yeshivoth*, (where one of his teachers was the last of the great talmudic casuists, R. Pinhas Hurwitz), became the famous Rabbi of Pressburg in Hungary and the founder of its great *yeshivah*, and impressed the stamp of his powerful personality not only on the orthodox communities of Hungary, but also on the immigration of Hungarian Jews to Palestine and on the whole struggle against the Reform movement in Judaism everywhere. Again, the devoted band of scholars who founded and built up the "Science of Judaism" were scattered over many lands and sometimes even wrote in different languages. Yet they succeeded in forming a single, closely knit group, and the spirit of cooperation with which all their work is infused obliterated the distances and differences between them. Indeed, the intensity and intimacy of this "spiritual communication" are truly remarkable.[49]

An interesting example of this spiritual communication between the various parts of world Jewry, which continued right down to modern times, is provided by the life story of David Sassoon. This banker from Baghdad, an observant Jew of distinguished lineage, made his money in

Bombay when his sons had already settled in London and, being himself something of a scholar, built a Jewish school in Bombay for which he wanted to publish suitable Hebrew textbooks and readers. Through the good offices of the writer and scholar Abraham Benisch, a native of Moravia and a member of the first Jewish Nationalist Students' Association (*Ahdut*), who had settled in London and was the editor of the *Jewish Chronicle*, the work of preparing these books was entrusted to Benisch's friend and fellow-townsman Moritz Steinschneider, the famous bibliographer, who was then living in Berlin. One of the texts published by Steinschneider, *Mashal u-Melitsa*, consists in part of the fables of J. L. Gordon, the famous Lithuanian Jewish poet of the *Haskalah*.

These few examples have purposely been taken from the period before the mass migration of Jews which brought together the different communities of the Diaspora, and before the rise of the Zionist movement which consciously set itself the aim of unifying the Jewish people as the first necessary step to its cultural and national renascence and the restoration of its political independence. Nor have the examples been drawn from periods when, as a result of systematic persecutions and blood libels, there was a general awakening of national consciousness throughout Jewry, when the feeling that "all Israel are brothers" became particularly strong and every Jew's readiness to aid his fellows was so often an outward expression of the sense of a common Jewish destiny. The illustrations that have been given will, I think, suffice to show that the spiritual interaction of the communities of the Diaspora continued down into the modern era, and in fact formed the basis of that living unity of the spirit, that

"Jewish climate" which, though greatly reduced in scope and depth in modern times, never ceased to be an independent, self-sustaining reality.

VIII

The living Jewish sense of unity which continued down into modern times thus resulted, as we have seen, from the fact that all Jews, as it were, breathed the same spiritual atmosphere. The concrete organizational framework of this unity was actually so tenuous as to be hardly felt at all. The Jewish community had ceased to be capable of organizing its own group existence. It no longer had the power to maintain the distinctive character of Jewish life even in a greatly reduced form, let alone in its entirety. Even Judaism itself, the faith which had once served every thinking Jew as his guide in life and had imposed an orderly pattern upon the inner world of his spirit, now lost its authority, as the part played by it in the spiritual life of the individual Jew was steadily whittled away. Every Jew could now arrive at his own set of values and beliefs without deciding his attitude to the whole self-contained system of Jewish doctrine, often without even knowing of the existence or nature of such a system. As for "world Jewry," its very existence as a social phenomenon seems highly disputable. The reason for this is not its lack of a concrete, fixed organizational framework, but rather its purely spiritual nature—its being nothing more than an emotional awareness which is aroused and makes itself felt only spasmodically, in times of crisis and calamity, and

lies dormant during the intervening periods. This absence
of any steady continuity in the life of world Jewry in
modern times makes it appear that modern Jewish history
is, in the main, simply the story of the deeds, successes
and failures of individual Jews, or Jewish families, or social
groups, and not the history of a whole community united
by certain living bonds. It would seem, therefore, that, for
the proper understanding of modern Jewish history, we
must first examine the reciprocal relations existing between
Jews, Judaism and world Jewry in this period.

There is no doubt that one of the most important
processes in Jewish history in modern times has been the
freeing of the individual Jew from the strict supervision
and control of the Jewish community. The community
was now no longer responsible for the civic conduct of
the individual, nor was it called upon to supervise the individual's performance of his obligations to the state and its
citizens. Conversely, the individual Jew no longer looked
to the community to guard his rights and protect his personal interests. Every single Jew was now a full citizen of
the state. Every single Jew could—in accordance with his
views, tendencies and interests—find the correct way to
defend his own personal rights, and, if necessary, also
those of the whole Jewish community, with the cooperation of other citizens, both Jews and non-Jews. Indeed,
the Jewish community no longer had the legal right to
superintend the private life and religious conduct of the
individual Jew, whose relations with God were now his
own personal affair. The community could no longer force
him, as had formerly been the case, to lead a religious life
and observe the commandments of the Mosaic Law.[50]
Every individual was now entitled to choose his mode of

life, whether religious or not, according to his own outlook and opinions. With regard to the commandments and religious customs, laws and rituals of Judaism, every Jew might now select such as he pleased and the organized Jewish community had no right to interfere with his choice. One thing, however, must not be forgotten. It is true that this freeing of the individual Jew from the control of the Jewish community went hand in hand with the forging of closer ties between him and his new community —the secular state and its citizen body. But these two processes did not take place solely through the force of the new historical circumstances; they were also the result of a collective Jewish endeavor. To free the individual Jew from the control of the Jewish community required a determined effort by many members of that community. So much so that, in order to liberate himself from the collective authority of religious Jewry, the individual had to act as part of another corporate Jewish body. This latter was, to all appearances, entirely new and its social bonds were extremely tenuous in fact as well as in theory. Nevertheless, it was bound, by the nature of things, to be a direct continuation of the organized Jewish community of the past, and particularly of just those elements in it that constituted the innermost core of its vitality, since these contained the secret of that strength and tenacity of purpose which the modern Jew required for his collective struggle.

The same was true of the Jewish religion. The social and cultural assimilation of the Jews to their gentile environment was one of the processes which determined not only the spiritual character of the modern Jew, but also, to no small extent, the content and form of modern Juda-

123

ism. It is no mere coincidence that this modern period, which saw such a rich Jewish contribution to secular philosophical studies, was one of the most barren in the fields of Jewish philosophy.[51] Nevertheless, there was perhaps never a time in the whole of Jewish history when the average Jew gave so much thought to Judaism and its problems and made such an independent effort to re-define his own attitude to them. He was obliged either to react as a Jew, or knowingly and deliberately to deny his Jewishness—which also meant adopting a definite stand. For the most part the average educated Jew, living in a collective Jewish atmosphere, sought ways to defend and justify the separate existence of the Jews, both to the outside world and to the Jews themselves.

Hence it came about that, just at the time when Judaism as a distinctive Jewish way of life was being drastically whittled away and its validity more and more queried, these questions themselves became part of "Jewishness." There was perhaps never a time when the various aspects of Judaism were so much discussed, asked about and debated by ordinary Jews as in the modern period. Nor did theoretical studies and discussions of this kind ever play such an important part in bringing about a reevaluation of Judaism from within as they have done in modern times, from the polemical debates in the early days of *Hassidism* and the *Haskalah* down to the ideological disputes of the last generation.

From the historical and social standpoint, the importance of all this lies in the actual fact that fairly large sectors of the Jewish population united and organized themselves into factions and cliques, trends and parties, on the basis of views held in common about the nature of Judaism and about the past history and future destiny of the Jews. The extent of the unanimity with which these opinions were held may be deduced from their success in giving a new spiritual content to the Jewishness of these circles which embraced large parts of the Jewish people.[52] Thus the corporate body of Jewry continued, in modern times too, to be held together by ideological bonds; and Jewish self-awareness continued to be a factor of great importance in shaping the dynamic forces at work in the nation and in determining the direction to be taken by them.

Much the same is also true of world Jewry. The active part now played by the Jews in the social and political life of the nations in whose midst they lived set up social and political barriers between the Jewish communities of different lands. This process of assimilation further resulted in the political abilities and social talents of considerable sections of the Jewish population being directed into the channels of the secular state and its society. But, at the same time, this process also developed in large numbers of Jews a taste for political and social life, accustomed them to modern forms of social organization, and gave them a political and social education. As was only natural, this experience and education were put to use in the Jews' public and political struggle for their national status amongst the nations and their civic rights as citizens of the state,[53] and also in their endeavors to aid their persecuted, impoverished and backward brethren. It was by their experience in gentile society and their training in its politics that the Jews were made to realize that this assistance to their persecuted and despised fellow-Jews was also elementary self-aid. They learned that the persecution and humiliation of Jews could not, by their very nature, be confined to one country; that the traditional hatred of the Jews was a convenient and effective weapon for their opponents to use in any political and social struggle; and that there would always be "enterprising spirits" interested in taking full advantage of this tradition, especially when they saw how successfully it had been exploited in other countries.[54] It is true that "world Jewry," as some kind of organized body, did not exist in modern times, nor indeed in any other period of Jewish history in the Diaspora; until the foundation of the *Alliance Israélite Universelle* there had never been any world Jewish organization whatsoever. But world Jewry has always existed as a consciousness of "belonging" and as a sense of sharing a common destiny. Such has been its historical character in modern times too. Nor is there any doubt that, in this period, international Jewish organizations have been more numerous, more active, and more influential than at any other time in the history of Diaspora Judaism. These organizations are an organic part of that new Jewish social entity which has undergone such great changes in recent generations. They constitute the upper strands of those new social and national bonds which have been forged in the Jewish Diaspora in modern times, as a result of all the changes and upheavals that have so radically altered the whole character of Jewish life.

IX

The changed political situation of the Jews in modern times, together with the sharp differences that now made themselves felt in the character of Jewry and its aims, gave rise to fundamental contradictions in the very essence of Jewish life which were constantly being resolved and harmonized by the living sense of unity in the nation. These fundamental contradictions thus generated dynamic forces which propelled Jewish history along its special course.

These contradictions were of four kinds: cultural, spiritual, political, and social.

Culturally, there was a contradiction between two different types of "Jewishness"—the one proudly assertive of its distinctively Jewish character, the other self-effacingly assimilationist. At the one extreme, there was the maximum amount of real, solid Jewishness possible in the Diaspora: populous and close-packed Jewish communities, in townlets, towns and cities, with their own distinctive way of life; and individual Jews with the conscious self-esteem of men confident of the truth of their own view of the world, Jews whose thoroughgoing spiritual and social Jewishness and whose relative independence, though veiled in their relations with the gentile world, can be clearly discerned in their whole outlook and way of thinking, as well as in their reactions and behavior. And at the opposite extreme, in contrast to this, there was the minimum of tangible Jewishness: small Jewish communities with sparsely populated centers and only a vague semblance of a distinctively Jewish way of life, side by side with the highest possible degree of Jewish self-effacement; whole groups of Jews who contented themselves with the barest minimum of their ancestral heritage, who were often completely cut off from it or deliberately abandoned it, and sometimes actually spurned it with contempt. These Jews not only assimilated the culture of the nations in which they lived and carefully copied their manners, but sometimes even completely identified themselves with these nations and lost no opportunity of declaring and demonstrating this identification.

These two diametrically opposed types of Jewishness which, with all the various intermediate stages between them, could be seen emerging, and were sometimes already fully formed, in the eighteenth century, are the fundamental feature of the life and history of the Jews in the nineteenth century.

It was only at the end of this century, and in the twentieth, that the differences between the two contrasted extremes began to become increasingly blurred.

These two different types of Jewishness are usually referred to as "Eastern" and "Western" respectively. Although there is, broadly speaking, no doubt a large measure of truth in this definition, it is far from providing a full and accurate explanation of the historical content of this fundamental contradiction. These two type of Jewishness were cultural and historical phenomena, which were also connected with the social status and economic and cultural integration of certain strata of the Jewish population in the secular state and its life. Hence, "westernized" Eastern Jews and "easternized" Western Jews have not been rare occurrences in modern times. There continued to be in the West—right down to the end of the nineteenth century and in larger numbers than is usually supposed—Jewish congregations and even whole communities which, in their distinctive way of life and in the Jewish "temperature" of their whole being, were a living embodiment of the situation described in the opening line of Judah Halevi's famous poem: "I am in the West, but my heart is in the East." Moreover, at the end of the nine-teenth and the beginning of the present century new con-gregations arose in the West comprising masses of Jews whose Jewishness was very real indeed; and in more and more circles there was a growth of Jewish consciousness and pride which had a marked influence on life and cus-toms. Conversely, in the East certain parts of the upper strata of the nation had already in the second half of the nineteenth century been infected with the taint of Jewish self-effacement; and the actual Jewish content of the dis-tinctive Jewish way of life had declined steeply in the last two generations before the Second World War even among the masses of Eastern Jewry.

The way in which these contrasted types of Jewishness came into being and the factors which produced them are an essential and basic part of the "making" of Jewish his-tory. This whole development can be traced through all the changes that were continuously taking place in the character of the life of the individual Jew, in his code of conduct and domestic arrangements, in his professional occupation and his social status, in his schooling and edu-cational standard, in his knowledge of the Torah and in his religious beliefs, in the language which he was accus-tomed to use at home, in conversation with his fellows and in his personal and business letters, and in the books which he read and knew well. The combined effect of these separate changes slowly accumulated over the years, until it suddenly became clear that they had brought about a complete revolution in the character of the whole being of Judaism.

The spiritual contradictions were those between the vari-ous religious trends in Judaism which kept rabbinical and scholarly circles, and through them the whole Jewish public, in a state of intellectual and emotional ferment throughout the modern period. The first, but by no means the only contradiction here, is the most fundamental contrast of all—that between the two extreme camps in Judaism: on the one hand, an integral Judaism, closed off from the world and refusing to come to terms with reality, and continuing to demand full jurisdiction over the private and public life of the individual Jew; and, at the other extreme, Reform Judaism, willingly and consciously giving up much of the Jewish religious tradition, especially that very part of it which had molded the individual Jew's special way of life and fostered his national consciousness, and contenting itself in theory with an abstract religious doctrine based on philosophical principles, and in practice with virtually nothing more than this or that "point of Judaism."

However, this contrast, fundamental though it is, not only does not comprise all the spiritual and religious contradictions in modern Jewry, but is itself not even wholly confined to the spiritual and religious sphere, since in part, it overlaps the historico-cultural contradictions. The whittling away of Judaism was often not so much the outcome of new views and ideas, as the result of different codes of conduct and habits of life. This new Judaism was, in fact, "reduced" rather than "reformed," and its influence on the religious and spiritual development of the nation was minimal. Reform Judaism, on the contrary, had an important influence on the history of modern Jewry, and is a term that should therefore be given to what might also be called "Modern Judaism"—that is, Judaism as conceived by the Jew who had adopted modern

130

ways of thought and forms of consciousness, and had made himself familiar with the scientific achievements and philosophical theories of the modern world and tried to fashion his Jewish belief and practice accordingly. To this modern trend in Judaism belong not only followers of Geiger and his school, but also a long line of distinguished opponents of the "Reformers," from Mendelssohn to Zecariah Frankel, from Krochmal to Ahad Ha-am.

The fundamental and hotly debated contradictions between the different trends in Judaism made themselves felt in the constant efforts to define the limits of the transcendent and temporal elements in it—to distinguish between its "everlasting truths" and its "historical truths," between its universal and its politico-national elements, between the belief in one absolute and eternally valid act of divine revelation and the conception of God's will as repeatedly revealing itself in the spirit of the time,[55] between Israel as the People of the Torah and the Torah as the creation of Israel, and the like.[56]

The struggle between these basically conflicting views was not confined to individuals. It was fought out publicly throughout the communities of the Diaspora to the accompaniment of discussions and studies, clarifications and argumentations, debates and polemics which kept the Jewish world in a ferment and injected into it a constant stream of ideas and conceptions, thoughts and reactions which, passing from individual to individual and from group to group, resulted in the emergence of new spiritual trends in Judaism.

No less important and decisive than the contradictions between the opposing trends in Judaism were the differences of type within the trends themselves and in the

131

many intermediate stages between them. Within each of the two extreme camps—Orthodoxy and Reform—there were fundamental differences between, on the one hand, a Judaism that was vigorous, challenging and progressive and, on the other hand, a Judaism that had encased itself within the hard shell of an arid conservatism. The power of Orthodox Judaism not only to preserve the distinctive character of Jewish life, but at the same time to enhance its moral and religious quality, was frequently determined by its own character. And the ability of Reform Judaism to exercise a permanent, lasting spiritual influence in Jewish affairs also depended on the differences of type to be found within its ranks.

Such differences of type have been strikingly evident in Orthodox Jewry throughout modern times, right down to the present day. At the beginning of this period, Orthodoxy was divided into the opposing factions of the *Hassidim*—the followers of the Baal Shem Tov—and the *Mitnaggedim*—the followers of the Gaon of Vilna. Hassidism tried to win the individual Jew by its appeal to the purity of his soul and to all the elements of his human experience, and at the same time to raise his powers of spiritual concentration and the intensity of his religious fervour to such a pitch that his whole life—including even its most secular moments—became infused with sanctity and his daily routine was elevated into an endless series of acts of worship. The *Mitnaggedim*, on the other hand, aspired to restrain the naturally sinful impulses of man not only by the well-tried negative method of increasing the fear of punishment and insisting upon a more stringent observance of the distinction between sacred and profane, but also by more positive means: by fostering a

more impassioned and diligent study of the Law, by bringing about the religious and spiritual improvement of the
individual Jew through his devoted self-absorption in the
profundities of talmudic knowledge, and by encouraging
the spread of that knowledge throughout the nation as a
whole.

In the nineteenth century, too, the forms taken by the
struggle between Orthodoxy and Reform were determined
by the differences within each of these religious trends.
Within the Orthodox camp there was, on the one hand, a
separatist faction that would have no truck with the "cove-
nant-breakers" in Jewry, regarding themselves as the only
true representatives of the traditional faith and openly
proclaiming themselves to be a separate religious sect completely divorced from the rest of the "Jewish community"
in the state.[57] But there was also a more moderate orthodoxy for which there could be no Torah without Israel.
To this orthodoxy, a world Jewry from which certain Jews
were excluded was like a Scroll of the Law from which
letters, words and even whole passages were missing, and
which was therefore regarded as unfit for religious use by
all shades of Jewish opinion.

A similar situation prevailed within Reform Judaism.
Jointly held doctrines were often applied in different ways,
according to the differences in the characters of the men
who held them. And the actual historical content of
jointly agreed upon practical religious reforms was determined solely by these differences. Both Mendelssohn and
Holdheim stressed the distinction that had to be made
between the "eternal truths" of Judaism (or "the religious
and human elements" contained in them "which are
equally valid at all times and in all places") and its "his-

torical truths" (or the national element in Judaism which originated in the period of the Jews' political independence as a nation).[58] But the conclusions drawn from this distinction varied with the different characters of those who drew them. Some of the Reformers deduced from this that the obligation of observing the practical commandments (*mitzvot*) was not dependent on their absolute truth, but on their being part of the tradition of the Jewish nation and on the Jews' will to belong to that nation. This school of thought maintained that the individual could not give up the observance of the *mitzvot*, which were the sole surviving form of religious ritual in modern Judaism, and at the same time remain a member of the Jewish nation. Others, however, inferred that the observance of the *mitzvot* was not an absolute religious obligation, since the *mitzvot* themselves were in the nature of rabbinical regulations which derived their validity from the particular circumstances of a given time and the consent of the contemporary Jewish community. There was also a third group that went so far as to maintain that the Jews were morally bound to abolish not only Jewish law, (the very existence of which, after the destruction of Jewish political independence, had become an anomaly), but also all the *mitzvot* that contained any relic of Jewish nationalism.[59]

As for the jointly agreed upon practical reforms, the dependence of their actual content on the particular ideological standpoint of their different advocators had already been pointed out by Zechariah Frankel at the Frankfurt Congress of Reform Rabbis (1845). To illustrate his contention, Frankel took the hypothetical question of whether the eating of leguminous plants should be permitted during the Passover, and showed that those who would permit it could be divided into two categories according to their reasons. In the first were those who, finding sanction for their opinion in the early legal authorities, did not recognize the right of later codifiers to impose such a prohibition on the whole community, while the second category consisted of those who obviously permitted the eating of leguminous plants during the Passover because they did not prohibit even the eating of leaven at that time.[60]

Even in the jointly formulated demands of modern Reform Judaism for a complete transformation of the economic structure of Jewry, and in its determined advocacy of a return to productive, and particularly agricultural, labor, there were differences of interpretation and emphasis. On the one hand, there were intellectuals and public workers who, while making every effort in both word and deed to strengthen the main supports of the existing economic structure of Jewry, at the same time strove to impress upon the Jews the need for setting their own house in order, for fear of the unfavorable impression that might be made on outside observers; and, on the other hand, there was a man like A. D. Gordon, who found the solution to the problem of creating a new, harmoniously integrated type of Jew and human being in an ethical theory based on the dignity of labor and a way of life lived in accordance with this principle.

These differences within each of the two main schools of thought in Judaism were also hotly debated and, as a result of the ideas they generated, gave rise to new spiritual trends. And since these trends were historical media through which the various movements in Judaism and the differences in outlook and opinion of their adherents took shape, they must form the second main chapter in any account of modern Jewish history.

The economic and political contradictions mentioned

above found expression in the two opposed types of Jew that emerged in modern times—the one obedient and submissive, readily bowing to authority and resigned to his fate, yielding and pacific; the other recalcitrant and critical, ready to defy authority and challenge his fate, self-assertive and rebellious. Long generations of living as a persecuted and despoiled minority in foreign lands, surrounded by hatred and always in danger, deprived of the most elementary security and dependent on the protection and kindness of the secular authorities whose chattels they were, had taught the Jews "to seek the welfare of the state" and "not to intervene in the affairs of others." As a result, they were everywhere known for their loyalty to the state and its rulers and their ready submission to its authority.

The lesson inculcated by this long and bitter experience was further reinforced by the general religious teachings of Judaism, according to which the ordeals and sufferings of the Exile were God's punishment of His people; hence, the only way to lessen the severity of this punishment and find eternal redemption was to regard it as wholly deserved and "accept its torments with love." Submission to the secular authority thus became, in some sense, a logical sequel to submission to "the judgment of Heaven." This was also the reason why the unrest that was so rife within the various communities, on account of the frequently intense and very bitter social conflicts inside them, rarely went beyond organized expressions of discontent, moral indictments, and propaganda for the presentation of soberly worded petitions to the secular authorities against the despotic rule of the communal oligarchy.[61] The domestic opposition in Jewry, in all its various guises and

136

forms, was always restrained by the feeling common to the whole Jewish community of being in "exile and captivity" and "exposed to humiliation by the enemy," so that every moment of Jewish existence became a dangerous emergency which could only be survived by carefully preserving the inner unity of the nation.

From the beginning of the modern era down to the present day, however, certain basic transformations have gradually and steadily taken place both in the situation of the Jews in the gentile states, and in their own outlook and mood. In the gentile states the stability of the "ruling power" was seriously shaken. It now ceased to be identical with the state itself, and became in principle—and in most cases, to a greater or lesser extent, in practice too—dependent on the consent of the citizens; indeed, it was sometimes even elected by them and exercised its authority only with their express permission. The citizen body thus became an organic part of the "ruling power." But the "natural rights" of man, which were the basis of the right of every citizen to take part in the government and supervise its functioning, also included the Jews. Hence the Jew was as much part of the "ruling power" as any other citizen of the state; so that when the Jew called for political reforms designed to ensure the freedom and equality of all citizens and to tighten the democratic control of the governmental authorities, so as to prevent them from slipping back into their bad old ways and to make them faithfully perform their proper functions, he was in fact merely carrying out his civic duty and loyally making his contribution to the realization of the ideals of the gentile nations, which was indeed the reason why he had been admitted into their reorganized society. Active participation in revolutions and other movements for the liquidation of "reactionary regimes," with their deeply ingrained traditions of oppression and habitual methods of extortion and discrimination, was also regarded by the modern Jew as a demonstration of his civic concern for "the welfare of the state," which was identical with "the welfare of the nations."[62]

The whole outlook of the individual Jew also underwent a profound change. The new Jew would not, and could not, look upon every misfortune to which he was subjected and every act of oppression and extortion perpetrated against him as the fully deserved "judgment of heaven." His new sense of vitality would no longer permit him to regard the resigned acceptance of suffering and torments as the way to redemption. His secular education and practical experience in social and political affairs had taught him to place the responsibility for anti-Jewish acts squarely on the shoulders of their instigators; and the new political and social framework made it possible for him to fight against these hostile forces by actively joining the rest of the citizen body in its revolt against the evils of a despotic regime. It must be admitted, however, that this Jewish element was largely subconscious and, in particular, was not overtly recognized by the Jewish revolutionaries, from the liberals and radicals to the socialists and communists among them, as a factor in their political activity. They preferred to say nothing at all about this whole aspect of the matter, or at least to gloss over it. This was the attitude that they adopted, consciously or unconsciously, in all their public appearances, on the assumption—which was sometimes expressly stated—that "the Jewish question" constituted only one small item in the great human and political struggle in which they were taking part.[63]

Nevertheless, the very fact that Jews were now participating in political life (and very frequently on the side of the "opposition" to the established regime) gave a militant character to the demands made by them in defense of their own rights as Jews, demands which were always based on legal and constitutional principles. The ruling classes, especially in the countries of central and eastern Europe, who were traditionally unfriendly to the Jews and for whom it was much more convenient to have them continue with their age-long habits of submissive obedience, naturally looked upon their readiness to fight for their rights as subversive in the extreme. This new Jewish militancy was thus organically bound up with the entry of the Jews into the civic, social and political life of the countries and states in which they were living. As the different sections of the Jewish population were accepted, one after the other, into the cultural and social life of the state, they also took up their positions on the battle-field of the struggle for equal Jewish rights and were filled with a new spirit of defiance. This is the spirit that was displayed throughout modern Jewish history, in the calm and reasoned apologetics of Mendelssohn no less than in the forcefully worded demands presented to the Prussian authorities by the members of the Berlin congregation, through their leading representatives, for the improvement of their status at the end of the eighteenth and in the middle of the nineteenth centuries; in the bold and astute articles explaining the Jewish case and proving its justice and in the strong and effective petitions and protests written by *Maskilim* in various countries, as well as in the

139

proud, unflinching stand adopted by Jewish representatives in the parliaments of the nations—as, for example, by Lionel de Rothschild in his struggle for the right to sit in the British House of Commons, despite his refusal to take the required Christian form of oath. At the end of the nineteenth and the beginning of the twentieth centuries, this new Jewish spirit of defiance showed itself in the political demonstrations and strikes by masses of Jewish workers living in the Pale of Settlement, and in the organized activities of the Jewish revolutionary parties (the *Bund*) whose ranks were firmly welded together by the pressure of the intolerable social conditions of Jewish life.

This spirit of defiant struggle penetrated right to the heart of Jewry and affected every single Jew. The living unity of the nation sent it pulsing into every sphere of the life of the Jewish masses throughout modern times, from the eighteenth century down to the present day. In eastern Europe, in the eighteenth century, it led to an uprising of artisans' guilds against the communal leaders and their arbitrary and corrupt rule of exploitation and barefaced robbery; it aroused the unlearned and simple masses against the spiritually arrogant rabbis who had imposed their authority on the community; and it brought the bolder spirits amongst the struggling and penniless scholars of the Law out in revolt against the established and privileged rabbinate which was hand in glove with the corrupt lay leadership. In western Europe, this same spirit placed the communal leadership in the hands of the rich and "progressive" Jewish bourgeoisie, the friends of the *Haskalah* movement, and thus increased the communal influence of the *Maskilim*, while reducing the importance of the rabbinate and limiting the scope of its jurisdiction.

ISRAEL AND THE DIASPORA

With the intensification of the social conflicts in the large Jewish populations of the great cities of eastern Europe and America at the end of the nineteenth and the beginning of the present century, this spirit of revolt became the driving force of the Jewish masses there. It roused them to action and welded them together for a long and courageous social and political struggle which, besides improving their economic condition and raising their cultural level, made them into an important factor in the social, cultural and political life of the nation. However, the most complete and most lasting outward expression of this constructive spirit of defiance was the "revolt against the *Galut*" which, in fact, has constituted the whole content of Jewish life in the last two generations, and the first indications of which mark the beginning of the modern era of Jewish history. This revolt, which drew its strength both from the heroic traditions of the nation's past and from the innermost yearnings of the individual Jew, combined the raging revolutionary fury that uproots old values and sweeps away established orders with the enthusiastic fervor and constructive energy that rebuild countries and renew peoples. The revolt against the *Galut* was like a huge river into which flowed all the smaller streams and tributaries of the Jewish struggle down the ages. It incorporated into itself all the various forms taken by that centuries-old struggle and all the various methods of resistance ever adopted by the Jews against their oppressors and persecutors, together with the stubborn persistence displayed by them in their hard struggle for survival and all the accumulated energy of their ardent yearning "to rebuild their own Land and to be rebuilt in it" which had been forcibly denied outlet during their

141

long generations of hard labor building for others through-out the world, as they had once built Pithom and Raamses for Pharaoh. The torchbearers of this revolt seemed, at first, to be only a few "faithful remnants," the thinly scat-tered members of a kind of underground movement whose whole existence was, so to speak, purely marginal to the mainstream of modern Jewish history. The course of this mainstream flowed through the movements for Enlighten-ment and Emancipation, the firm establishment of the Jews in their countries of residence, and their integration into the cultural and social life of the gentile nations. But this course was by no means easy and straightforward. Every point along it had to be bitterly fought for in an exhausting struggle full of historical insult for the nation as a whole and personal humiliation for many of its in-dividual members. The individual Jew was deeply wounded by the necessity of once again having to prove his equal worth as a human being and his value as a citizen, and of once more having to demand what was only his elementary civic right—namely, the acceptance and public proclama-tion of his equality, and the constitutional recognition of his full citizenship and its legal formulation. But even when that point had been gained, he still had to make sure that all these proclamations, "recognitions," laws and statutes concerning the Jews were fully honored in practice. And sometimes he had to protest vigorously against the whole tendency of the "pestered" bureaucratic machine to disregard Jewish constitutional rights.[64]

It was in the course of this struggle that the first sparks of the great Jewish revolt of modern times were struck. Carried by the living unity of the dispersed nation to all parts of the Diaspora, they here and there set hearts and spirits aflame. Little by little the features of the new, defiant type of Jew began to take shape. Some of these sparks of revolt lighted the passionate devotion with which young Jewish scholars now applied themselves to the study of Jewish history and the spiritual legacy of Jewry, with the avowed aim of demonstrating the nation's historical continuity and the unity of its culture (Zunz and Graetz). Others inspired the remarkable love for the Hebrew language felt by the Jewish *Maskilim* (A. D. Lebenson, Mapu, J. L. Gordon) and the devoted efforts made by them to free the "beautiful tongue," the relic of past Jewish glories. But their most striking effect was seen in the renewed activity of the last faithful remnants of the old messianic visionaries, men who had never ceased to dream of the Return to Zion and whose dreams now took on a modern guise (Alkalay, Kalischer) and began to be filled with a yearning for the spiritual and social revival of the nation, as well as for its physical redemption. Sometimes this yearning was the secular idealism of utopian social reformers who had already tried, and failed, to impose their own ideal conceptions of society on the gentile world (Hess);[65] and sometimes it was the passionate longing of devoutly orthodox Jews, wearied by the ineffectiveness of their stubborn efforts to preserve their religious inheritance intact in an environment swept by the winds of contemporary disbelief and assimilation, in which there was no central Jewish authority strong enough to impose the general will of the whole community on the individual Jew (Schlesinger).[66]

In either of these two latter forms, the promise of deliverance held out to the nation by the new messianic visions was of the kind likely to weaken its revolutionary ardor. Nevertheless, in Smolenskin's impassioned call for the strengthening of Jewry everywhere, and in his fiercely critical speeches and articles, with their violent attacks on the whole course of modern Jewish history, the rumble of the approaching Jewish revolt can be clearly heard— even though the tidings of redemption reached only a few ears, and small though the response to Smolenskin's call was. Those who heard the tidings and answered the call may have been few in number, but they were the men of the future, steadfast in spirit and young in years. Ben Yehuda's clearly reasoned demand for the revival of the Hebrew language as a prerequisite to the national rena-scence of Jewry, his insistence on the strengthening and reinforcing of the *Yishuv* as a necessary preliminary to the restoration of Jewish political independence, and his own putting into practice of what he preached by immigrating to Palestine were all clear signs of a profound change in the whole outlook of these important, albeit limited, cir-cles of Jewish youth.

Still, the first stirrings of the revolutionary spirit among Jewish youth would perhaps never have burst out into the full-scale revolt of the *Hibbat Zion* movement against the *Galut* had it not been for the relentless "war" against the Jews declared by the forces of anti-Semitism, a war waged with all the organized armory of traditional hostility and deliberate incitement, social opposition and cultural rejection, economic rivalry and political calculation, re-ligious bigotry and racial hatred, narrow nationalism and human degeneracy. This *Hibbat Zion* revolt, which was kindled in the early eighties of the last century, was still far from being an uprising of the whole nation. But hun-dreds of Jews were actively involved in it right from the start, and thousands and tens of thousands of others were roused and attracted by it. From the very beginning this revolt had all of the qualities necessary to transform it into the great national Zionist movement which, with the historical changes wrought by it on the Jewish people and its ancient land and its tremendous impact on the whole of Jewish life, comprises practically the whole of Jewish history in the last two generations. With the spread and intensification of the war against the Jews, the Jewish national movement also grew stronger and wider, as more and more sections of Jewry joined its ranks. Moreover, as the rebuilding of Palestine progressed, and as the close ties between the people and its Land were renewed and strengthened and there gradually came into being a completely Jewish society created by the efforts of the Jewish masses, the movement of revolt took firmer root in the consciousness of the individual Jew and gave rise to a new Jewish type. So powerful was the impetus of the revolt against the *Galut* that it forced the historical course of the nation back into its original channels and recreated the character of the modern Jew in the likeness of his ancient ancestors. It was not only in the nation's outstanding figures—as in the extraordinary, almost legendary, personality of Herzl—that the ancient Israelite type was now revived. Its primary manifestations are to be found in all the forms of historical activity produced by the revolt against the *Galut*: in the members of *Bilu* and the men of the Second Aliyah, in pioneers and illegal immigrants, in those who drained the marshes of Palestine and settled its wastelands, in settlement-builders and road-makers, in watchmen and defenders, in the men who revived the Hebrew language and renewed its culture.

Wherever the influence of the revolt against the *Galut* made itself felt, this new type arose—from the Jews who united in self-defense against pogroms and social and economic discrimination, to those who fought against the Nazis as partisans in the forests or defied them in the ghettos. The establishment of this particular type as *the* modern type of Jew resulted from the living unity of the whole Jewish nation, which smoothed away the contrasts and contradictions between the different existing Jewish types and blended them together.

This process was brought about by the political movements which gave expression to the contemporary Jewish awareness of the need for radical changes in the life of both the individual Jew and of the whole community, and to the desire for joint action based on a common recognition of the necessity of transforming and improving contemporary Jewish life. These movements were organizationally connected with certain ideologies resulting from the spiritual trends of the Diaspora and were set in the framework of the general historical processes that determine the naure of the changes in the conditions of human life.

The social contradictions are those between the actually existing Jewish society and its official organizational patterns. Jewish society in modern times was multiform, extremely complex and in a state of perpetual ferment; whereas its official organizational patterns were uniform, simple and in a condition of inner petrification. Officially, the state usually recognized the Jewish congregation in any given place as simply a religious community which was authorized to provide for the religious needs—including religious education—of its members, to supervise their conduct, and to manage their charitable institutions.[67] But there were some countries (like Russia) in which the state did not even recognize the existence of a religious congregation. In such cases, the only Jewish organizational unit was the synagogue and its officials; and these separate units combined to form a general Jewish organization known as the "Council of Synagogue Managements," which was from time to time summoned before the authorities, as the need arose, and was regarded by them, in both theory and practice, as the authorized representative Jewish body. The jurisdiction of the congregation was thus confined within narrow geographical limits and restricted to a small range of local Jewish affairs. The congregation was no longer empowered even to study and debate, let alone actively deal with, matters affecting the Jews throughout the state, still less those connected with "world Jewry." All these matters now came within the "unorganized area" of Jewish life, which grew steadily wider in modern times with every contradiction of the "organized area." The satisfaction of religious requirements frequently ceased to be a vital need for a large portion of the members of the congregation. Religious indifference spread to large sections of the Jewish public, while those who were spiritually alert to these problems and in whose life religion continued to play an important part were hopelessly disunited, both on account of the proliferation of different beliefs and opinions, and also through the attenuation of the common element in Jewish religious practice and the Jewish way of life. Belonging to the congregation, it is true, was still one of the things taken for granted. Generally speaking, every Jew was automatically a member of his congregation, unless he explicitly announced his withdrawal from it; and no Jew formally severed his connexions with his congregation, unless he intended, sooner or later, to abandon Judaism altogether. But, for all that, belonging to the congregation was, to a great extent, a passive fact rather than an active factor in the life of the individual Jew. The religious, spiritual and social ties which bound the members of the congregation together in a single organizational pattern were so greatly weakened that they sometimes lost their hold altogether. The new links that were forged in modern times did not find their social expression in the existing organizational patterns; indeed, the congregation did its best to prevent them from encroaching on its sphere. The congregation was thus no longer a uniform, all-embracing Jewish organization which could mold the common will of the whole Jewish community and crystallize its powers of concerted action for the realization of this agreed purpose. Even in countries where its organization was firmly established and enjoyed the recognition of the secular authorities, the congregation in modern times simply provided an official framework for a whole variety of Jewish social activities which organizationally had no real organic conection with each other. The mainstream of modern Jewish history bypassed the congregation, flowing through the channels of the special organizational forms created by the social movements and ideological trends of modern Jewry. It goes without saying that these forms too, like the movements and trends themselves, were conditioned by the changes and transformations taking place in the character and conditions of modern life. Jewish history in modern times was made directly by all the various Jewish circles and factions, societies and associations, groups and chapters, committees and unions, parties and federations which together molded the joint will of the Jewish community and consolidated its power of planned and concerted action for the attainment of social and national goals.[68]

X

The modern era of Jewish history began, as has already been explained, with the immigration of Rabbi Judah the Pious and his band of followers to Palestine in 1700, an event which, in all its fundamental aspects, symbolized the twilight of the Jewish Middle Ages and the birthpangs of a new epoch. The end of the modern era in Jewish history was ushered in by the 1947 resolution of the United Nations setting up a Jewish state in part of Palestine and was finally sealed by the declaration of the independent State of Israel on May 15, 1948. That moment marked the beginning of a great new chapter in Jewish annals, with "Israel in its land" once more about to take the center of the stage in the nation's history.

The modern era thus lasted approximately two hundred and fifty years. During this time there were two other noteworthy dates which also constitute turning points in the life and destiny of the Jewish nation in this period: the French Revolution and the First Emancipation of the Jews (1789); and the rise of modern anti-Semitism and the beginning of its unbridled onslaught on the Jews in Germany and tsarist Russia (1881).

Modern Jewish history may accordingly be divided into

the following three periods: 1700–1789, 1789–1881, 1881–1947. Each of these periods had its own distinctive character resulting from the following factors: a certain general historical framework which largely conditioned the historical course followed by the development of the Jewish nation in that period; characteristic demographic, economic, social and cultural processes which determined the basic quality of contemporary Jewish life; ideological trends peculiar to the period, which determined and gave expression to its distinctive spiritual character; new social movements which crystallized the joint will of world Jewry and gave it a sense of direction; and other organizational patterns by which the energies of the Jewish public were concentrated and channeled into deliberately chosen courses of action.

The first period, from 1700 to 1789, may be summed up as the period of Jewish territorial settlement, social disintegration and cultural awakening. These three tendencies were conditioned by the main elements of the general historical framework of the time: by the expansion and consolidation of state finances through the concerted efforts of the whole governmental machinery; by the delegation of the practical functions of government by absolute monarchies to a disciplined civil service, thereby freeing the regime from all direct class influence; and by the weakening of the social power and official influence of the Church, in pursuance of the aim of maintaining the personal freedom of the individual in all the spheres of the spirit, including religion. This general historical framework made it possible for the Jews to rise economically and advance socially in gentile society, increased the security of their lives and property, and enhanced the influence of the rich, leading and powerful members of the community. It also paved the way for closer social intercourse between Jewish and Christian circles, encouraged better cultural understanding between them, and aroused in many Jews the desire for a reexamination of their spiritual heritage in the light of their new approach to life.

Even in those countries (e.g. Poland) in which the attempt to establish these new principles of government was not wholly successful, and which consequently declined steadily throughout this period, the principles themselves nevertheless exercised so great an influence on the life of the nation that in the second half of the eighteenth century, when the social, political, economic and cultural struggle in these countries increased in intensity, it was carried on in this same general historical framework. Hence, the general trend of the changes and transformations in contemporary Jewish life was also in the direction of territorial consolidation and social disintegration: toward the establishment of Jewish settlements and their economic integration, and at the same time toward adaptation to the gentile environment through outward self-effacement combined with the domination of the community by the richer stratum of assimilated Jews.

This period was also one of spiritual awakening in Jewry. The contemporary trends and movements in Judaism were, it is true, sharply contrasted. There was, for example, a great difference between the enthusiastic religious revivalism of *Hassidim* in the Ukraine and Poland, and the movement of the Lithuanian *Mitnaggedim* for the strengthening of strict orthodoxy through the more intensive study of the Torah. And both these movements were a far cry from the new sense of worldliness acquired by a large portion of the younger generation of Jews as a result of the intellectual awakening of the *Haskalah*. Nevertheless, all these different trends and movements were alike in that they sprang from the contemporary spiritual ferment which, in one form or another, set them thinking afresh about the Jew's position in the world. While this ferment undoubtedly took much of its character from the general historical framework and from the changes in gentile society, its actual origin is to be traced back to the individual Jew's loss of faith in the aftermath of the failure of the Shabbethian messianic movement, a failure which involved the complete destruction of the world of medieval Jewish values. For most of this period this spiritual ferment was thus one of the causes of the organizational disintegration apparent everywhere in Jewry. But, toward the close of the period, when the various trends and movements in Judaism had each attained its own clearly defined character, it became an integrating force which brought into being new forms of Jewish organization, above all the unified ideological groupings which have played such an important part in modern Jewish history.

The second period, from 1789 to 1881, can be defined as the period of civic equality, national dissolution and historical identification. These three trends were also conditioned by the main features of the contemporary historical setting: by its economic liberalism, which gave free play to individual initiative in all spheres of economic life; by its political democracy, which brought the citizens into active and permanent partnership in the political life of the state; and by the cultural nationalism which stamped all the manifestations of the spiritual life of the nations with its seal. The changes and transformations in

Jewish life during this period—even in countries like Russia, which seemingly went their own special way—were also set in this general historical framework. The free play and wide scope allowed to individual enterprise in the economic field were, through the practical development of the natural sciences, directed toward opening up the economic possibilities latent in every locality.

At the same time, the achievements of modern technology and the rationalization of labor, together with the striving for the maximum exploitation of regional economic potentialities and the astounding improvement in the internal means of communication, were instrumental in bringing about the economic unification of the various parts of the same country. The permanent territorial settlement of the Jews and their integration into the economies of their countries of residence were thus inextricably bound up with their active participation in the economic development of those countries. Democracy was, by its very nature, based on the active interest taken by the citizens in state affairs and on their ability to play an intelligent part in the political organization of the nation's life, in the shaping of the political regime best suited to its requirements and circumstances, and in the effective supervision of its needs. An essential feature of the democratic regime was, therefore, the uniform education of the masses to fit them for a larger share in the nation's historical and cultural heritage which had for centuries been mainly the privileged preserve of the small aristocratic minority. In this way, the economic consolidation of the various countries of Europe in the nineteenth century also led to the emergence of nationalist cultures, while the political emancipation of the Jews in the countries of the

Diaspora, and their cultural integration into the nations in whose midst they dwelt, were throughout contingent upon the development of democracy in Europe.

Those trends and movements in Judaism which openly rejected Jewish nationalism, and which advocated reforms in the Jewish religion in the spirit of this rejection, were also ideological expressions of the processes of national dissolution and religious adaptation directly resulting from the general trend toward cultural homogeneity which gave the Jews too the feeling of being partners in the historical heritage of the gentile nations and of sharing in their national identity.

Yet, at the same time, the special historical character of these popular national cultures also set limits to the processes of cultural assimilation and national dissolution among the Jews. The Jewish past, historically and culturally, had too strong a reality, both in the innermost consciousness of the individual Jew and in the collective awareness of the gentile nations, for it to be possible to escape from it, ignore it, or blur its outlines by any amount of cultural assimilation. Moreover, this past had also entered deeply into the histories of other nations, and the marks left on the memories of these nations by this interlocking of historical destinies were not of the kind calculated to help forward the civic emancipation and cultural assimilation of the Jews. In relation to the past, therefore, such assimilation was out of the question; indeed, it was in glaring contradiction to the whole process of civic emancipation.

The more thoughtful of the Jewish intellectuals were thus forced to seek a closer identification with their own past. In so doing, they gained a greater appreciation of its historical importance, and began striving to inculcate a general awareness of its equal value culturally with the legacy of other nations. This process of historical identification with the Jewish past was accelerated above all by the joint struggle which the Jews were continually obliged to wage against their antagonists who, relying on the centuries-old tradition of anti-Semitic contempt and hatred, placed every possible obstacle in the way of the Jews' attainment of civic equality.

Jewish life in eastern Europe was also set in this historical framework. And the same processes, broadly speaking, occurred even in Russia, the state in which there was the densest concentration of Jews and where Jewish life was most real and intense. In Russia, however, the Jews' new worldly ambitions could not follow the path of cultural assimilation to the gentile environment, since the still emergent culture of their neighbors had as yet no uniform, independent character, nor was it always identical with the political and economic development in which the Jews were involved. Thus the identification of the largest Jewish community with its past was also intensified during this period by the fact that its greater secular knowledge and its new sense of worldliness were achived through a strengthening of Jewish consciousness and a process of self-regeneration which gave a truly Jewish character to its new orientation to the world (as seen in the new Hebrew literature). Hence, the end of this period saw the creation of novel forms of Jewish social cohesion (such as the *Alliance Israélite Universelle*) which were imbued with a spirit of Jewish historical self-recognition.

The third phase of modern Jewish history, from 1881 to 1947, may be defined as the period of political revolt, of the organization of the Jewish masses for self-defense, and of the strengthening of Jewish nationalism. The general trend of this phase was determined by the "war against the Jews" declared at the beginning of the period and waged unceasingly right down to its end. This war, with all its fluctuating vicissitudes, was set in the general historical framework of a strife-torn world. This was a world which saw the rise and fall of classes in a bitter conflict over living standards, social status, and political power; the struggle for mastery between emergent and effete parties fighting for popular influence and political domination; the clash between declining old-established nations, with their long experience of despotic rule, and the revolutionary force of rising new nations—the former defending their centuries-old positions of strength and stubbornly refusing to surrender the last relics of their power, the latter rising in revolt against their foreign overlords and fanatically striving to eliminate every trace of alien influence from their fatherlands; wars between states—large and small, old and new, strong and weak—which even in periods of peace carried on a saber-rattling propaganda battle in defense of their vital interests and legal rights; and rivalry for the division and control of the world between great power blocs which, for all the vast sweep of their political calculations, knew how to take account of every force, no matter how small or apparently insignificant, that could be made to serve their purposes.

Within this historical framework every aspect of human life became a battlefield.

Economically, this was in all countries a period of rapid industrialization, of vast accumulations of capital in the leading banks, of the concentration of business in departmental stores and the like, and of the nationalization of whole sectors of the state's economy. All these developments led to the social decline of large sections of the nation and the creation of mass urban populations, heightened the tension of the rivalry between different individuals and groups in the nation and offered greater opportunities for its exploitation, made the working classes into a political force, and prepared the way for the effective influence of organized public bodies on economic life.

Politically there was a steady, irresistible expansion of direct governmental control and supervision, and a correspondingly progressive contraction of the spheres of life outside the jurisdiction of the state. With the constant increase in the power of the bureaucratic administrative machine, the struggle for the control of this new juggernaut became ever more intense. Popular participation in political life was now no longer a theoretical and constitutional question, but a determining factor in the rise and fall of governments. The whole period was one of transition from old to new regimes. The old guard—the upper classes of society with their age-long traditions of ruling and of diplomatic etiquette—yielded its place, sometimes with a struggle, but sometimes also by adapting itself to the new conventions, to the new forces. Some of these latter burst onto the scene with all the overwhelming impetus of an unbridled lust for power while others gradually established themselves by quietly infiltrating into the ranks of the old order and by becoming associated with it, wholly or in part, in the responsibilities of government. This political development intensified the class war and the party struggle, thus making the whole period one of violent social and political upheavals. The stability of the existing regimes was shaken with varying degrees of violence, and the whole of society was in a state of seething discontent.

In this general atmosphere there was little room for humanitarianism in political philosophies and social relations. As a result of the material successes of society (which were now set up as the primary moral principle in human life) and the contraction of its spiritual content, moral responsibility was transferred from the single individual to the whole community. The efficient application of scientific methods to the mass-organization of modern society, and the constant demagogic exploitation of the baser human instincts and passions as a weapon in the social struggle, brought about a steep decline in the intellectual and moral standards of the ordinary man in this period. The jungle law of "might is right" more and more prevailed, not only in the social relations between weaker and stronger elements within any one state and nation, but also in international affairs. The "war against the Jews" was thus an integral part of this general historical and cultural atmosphere. It provided an outlet for the bitterness of the social déclassés; it was an effective means of restoring the fortunes of the Jews' unsuccessful economic rivals; and it was also a satisfactory way of deflecting the wrath of the masses in the political struggle from its true object. And also it served as a kind of cesspool into which could be poured all the moral corruption of a decaying society.

This violent and ruthless anti-Semitic onslaught determined the course taken by the changes which occurred during this period in Jewish life, within the setting of the general historical framework. All these changes were in the direction of self-defense, social revolt, and increasing nationalism. The Jews were able to survive in this period only by being constantly ready to defend themselves; and the power of this self-defense lay not only in the feeling displayed by the individual Jew for the human suffering of his fellow-Jews, but still more in the popular extent of this feeling, which was a direct expression of the sense of being involved in a harsh common destiny. This sense was in fact shared by all the Jews of the time, even though they sometimes tried to dismiss it from their consciousness. The spontaneous, mass nature of this Jewish organization for self-defense remained plainly and irrefutably evident, despite the attempts of "leaders" and "scholars" to explain to "the world" that this interest displayed by the Jews in the fate of their brethren was in no way different from the interest taken by the members of any other creed in the fate of their coreligionists.[69]

Indeed, the all-embracing mass character of this self-defense made it impossible to conceal from the Jewish public that it was, in fact, socially isolated in its struggle for survival in this period. Hence the social and political revolt of the younger generation of Jews. Although this revolt was not, it is true, always directed against the general plight of the Jews, there is no doubt that this plight was one of the most important factors in bringing it about. The part played by the contemporary revolutionary ferment in Jewry in determining the character of modern Jewish life is in no way lessened by the fact that this spirit of revolt was only rarely openly displayed. The spontaneous organization of the Jewish masses for self-defense was set in motion by a completely or partially hidden spirit of social and political revolt, arising from a sense of isolation

and utter self-dependence. This compelled the Jews to
devise political forms and methods of their own, and to
create organizational patterns specially suited to the Jewish
capacity for concerted action. In this way, the independence of the Jews in public affairs steadily increased
throughout this period. Their punctilious observance of
the general legal and social framework in which these
organizational patterns were set merely served to empha-
size their complete independence in their own aims and
in their methods of attaining them. This was how the
historical tendencies of this period became part of the
daily life of both the Jewish community as a whole and
of its individual members.

The same tendencies were also at work in the vast movement of Jewish migration which scattered Jewish communities over all the countries of the globe and led to the
concentration of large masses of Jews in the great cities
of the world. These tendencies had a profound influence
on the stubborn resistance offered by the Jews to all attempts to dislodge them from their social and economic
positions in the gentile world; and they played a large
part in arousing the class consciousness and cultural awareness of the Jewish masses, and in their organization as a
political force. They also left their mark on the contemporary social trends and movements in Judaism. While in
some of these the element of defense was most prominent,
in others the main emphasis was placed on the strengthening of Jewish nationalism: on renewed cooperation between all classes for civil defense; on a wide-spreading
cultural revival drawing its strength from a close adherence
to the primary literary sources of the nation, together with
an enthusiastic appreciation of the recent creations of

Jewish folk art; on a bold revolutionary bid for cooperation with all the other movements for political and social reform in the world; and on a determined, unflagging drive for national and political liberation through the Jews' own constructive efforts, accompanied by a renewal of the character of the individual Jew and a regeneration of Jewish society.

These trends and movements also created new organs for themselves—new both in aim and in form: parties and federations, political organizations and cultural associations, institutions and undertakings, which, taken all together, were the outward expression of the reunification of Jewry into a national political body aiming at the territorial concentration of the Jews on the soil of their ancestors and the attainment of their political independence in their ancient fatherland.

BOOK
III

THE
REBIRTH
OF ISRAEL

ISRAEL AND THE DIASPORA

I

By the term "rebirth of Israel" I do not mean to imply merely its rebirth as a state, or even those basic factors which constitute this political rebirth. There are those who date this political rebirth from November 29, 1947, the day of the United Nations' decision to partition Palestine and establish in one of the partitioned areas a Jewish state; and there are others who date it from the Declaration of the fifth of *Iyar*, 5708 (May 14, 1948), concerning the establishment of the State of Israel. To the first of these two events, or to both together, are attached the subsequent Arab invasions and the Jewish victories which culminated in armistice agreements with the Arab states, and the recognition by the international community of nations of Israel's independence, which found its full expression in the admittance of Israel to the United Nations. And there are those who add the awakening of multitudes of Jews in the Diaspora and the Ingathering of the Exiles —two events which manifested the recognition of the State of Israel on the part of the Jewish people—as being at least a partial fulfillment of the hopes of many generations for Redemption and deliverance.

However, these significant events, if taken by themselves, do not at all reveal the true essence of the rebirth of Israel, for they are only the expression and revelation of this rebirth. Its essence lies in an altogether different factor, namely, in the emergence of a large Jewish settlement in the country, a settlement which struck roots in the land and built an independent economy tied to the land and its natural characteristics; which established a new unified and consolidated Jewish society; which revived the Hebrew language, and invested the life of the community with renewed national-territorial-cultural foundations; and which showed ability to govern its own affairs, to set its own life in order, and to protect itself against its enemies.

Seventy-two years ago, approximately 22,000 to 24,000 Jews lived in Israel, the vast majority in the four cities which were called "Four Lands": Jerusalem, Hebron, Tiberias, and Safed. A very small minority lived in tiny communities in the coastal cities of Jaffa, Haifa, Acre, and Gaza. In a few other cities, such as Shefaram and Shechem, there were also a few Jewish families. The majority of this Jewish settlement was without economic roots, lived on monetary donations from abroad, and played virtually no part in the economy of the land or in its meager productivity, being only consumers. Even from a demographic point of view, this was not a settlement of wage earners, for an unusually large percentage were old men and women. The settlement was not consolidated; it was divided into communities and *Landsmannschaften*, each a world in itself. The settlers did not constitute an entity *per se*. They were divided into groups according to their places of origin, and generally maintained past ties, spoke different languages, and were distinct not only as citizens of different countries but also in ways of life. The Jewish settlers were far from modern culture and seemed to be remnants of an historical phenomenon concentrated in a distant corner on the edge of the vast expanse of Jewish existence.

The following deals essentially with sixty-five years, 1882–1947. During the thirty-two years between the first settlement and the First World War, the *Yishuv*, the

166

settlement of Jews in the Land of Israel, multiplied three and a half times (to 84,000 persons), and the number of settled communities grew from eight to fifty-four, forty-four of them agricultural. The proportion of the Jewish population to the total increased from approximately 4.5 per cent to 12 per cent. Within the *Yishuv* itself, the proportion of Jews settled in villages rose to 14 per cent.

During the thirty-three years which followed (1914–1947) the *Yishuv* increased more than seven and a half times (to 643,000). The number of communities and settlements rose to 330, 302 of them agricultural; the proportion of the Jewish to the total population rose to 33 per cent, and the proportion of Jews settled in villages rose to 25.6 per cent (165,000). At the beginning of the Jewish resettlement, the proportion of Jews in the *Yishuv* to Jews in the rest of the world was 0.18 per cent; in 1947, it was approximately 6.3 per cent. Though the *Yishuv* possessed only 7 per cent of the total land of Palestine (within the boundaries of the "national home") it succeeded in establishing an independent economy which constituted a separate economic unit and which fixed permanently the nature and character of the country. The proportion of Jewish settlements to that of all other settlements was 27.3 per cent; and though the proportion of grain products raised by Jews was not more than 8 per cent, in other fields of agriculture their proportions were high: 25 per cent in greens, 50 per cent in citrus, 89 per cent in fodder and herbage. The Jewish share in industry and trades, which began to play a significant role in the country's economy, was about 84 per cent, or—according to the value of industrial production and the number of people gainfully employed in it—about 88 per cent.

All of this economic and communal upbuilding was

done by the Jews themselves: with their labor and their money, with their organizational ability, and with the strength of their ideals. They formed an independent economic entity in the country, as well as an organized unit of people who toiled zealously to build up the country and promote the development of the *Yishuv*, to better their lives, to raise their standard of living and their social status, to meet the colonization requirements of the *Yishuv*, and to protect it against the outside forces always conspiring against it.

The *Yishuv* also succeeded in consolidating itself culturally. It not only established a complete system of education, from kindergarten to the Technion and the University, which encompassed almost the entire *Yishuv*, but remarkably it also succeeded in unifying itself through the Hebrew language. The Hebrew language became the living language of the masses, the language of the educational system, of the culture, the learning, and the science—and also the *official language* of the people.

All these events together constitute *the rebirth of Israel.* Only on the basis of these fundamental factors did the United Nations decide to establish a Jewish state in a portion of the Land of Israel. The fundamental importance of the *Yishuv* in the creation of the state was made fully apparent with the Declaration of Independence and revealed itself in the War of Independence, and the nations of the world took full cognizance of it when they decided to admit Israel to the United Nations.

In other words, the political rebirth of Israel is a direct result of the resettlement of Israel in its own land: within sixty-five years there arose a Jewish settlement, whose progress, growth, and expansion embodied and interwove elements which brought about its crystallization as a seedling people and a fledgling state, and thus made it the bearer of Israeli independence. This growth and expansion of the *Yishuv* is deliberately called "the resettlement of Israel in its own land," because this term expresses fully the unique historical character of the formation of the new settlement.

II

I shall try first to explain the meaning of my definition of the rebirth of Israel, and then to establish its veracity.

The historical foundations of this rebirth comprise those forces and elements operative in the formation of the *Yishuv* that resulted from the endeavors of previous generations. During the formation of the *Yishuv* such historical factors already existed.

The formation of the *Yishuv*, its growth to the status of a seedling people and bearer of Israeli independence, is undoubtedly one of the most remarkable chapters not only in the history of the Jewish people but in the history of civilization. The essence of this phenomenon can best be defined and understood by describing the formation of the new settlement as "the resettlement of Israel in its own land." The term "settlement" in Hebrew denotes permanent settlement in a specific land, identification with it, and self-rule. It implies not merely settlement but permanent settlement born out of a realization of continuous possession, of ownership. Because of this, settlement, in the language of the Bible, is always used in terms of a family, a tribe, or a nation. "Settlement" then has, as an essential part of its meaning, a taking hold which contains something of permanence, of duration, of the will to own and control. Every act of settlement has within itself an element of the eternal.

The formation of the *Yishuv* was not merely a socio-economic process—not merely the result of the fact that Jews, suffering in the places where they dwelt, decided to emigrate from the countries of their fathers to where living conditions were better, where there was greater security and opportunity to earn a livelihood. The formation of the *Yishuv* was also the result of political, social, spiritual, and moral processes.

The true significance of the resettlement was that the acquisition of the soil was intimately tied to a complete renewal of social and psychological experiences. This resettlement in the homeland could be accomplished only through laying bare the basic instincts which bind man to the soil and which are hidden in the recesses of his being, and through their renewal as a primary force in the crystallization of a society and in the emergence of a people. It is understandable that this renewal was, by its very nature, bound to influence, to a great degree, both the individual who had already settled in the country and the new society which arose there. In this process of resettlement there was naturally embodied a great human drive for the spiritual renewal of the individual, both through his intimate relationship to nature and to labor and also through his relationship to other individuals and to the community in everyday living.

The human drive embodied in and arising from this process was inherent in men and women permeated with

170

a sense of mission on behalf of the entire Jewish people. They regarded themselves and their endeavors, their efforts and their self-renewal, as an expression of generations of yearning, of the collective will of the Jewish people revealed and renewed in all its manifestations through the desire to return to Zion; they regarded themselves as the messengers of a people returned to its homeland. This aim of the resettlement achieved remarkably clear manifestation in every major and minor act associated with it. One need only recount the names of the groups and organizations established to acquire soil and promote immigration, or the names of the settlements: *Dabber 'el bnai Yisrael veyisau* (Speak unto the children of Israel, that they go forward—Exodus 14:15), *Bet Yaakob leku venelka* (O house of Jacob, come ye, and let us go—Isaiah 2:5), *Shearit Yisrael* (Remnant of Israel), *Mikveh Yisrael* (Ingathering of Israel), *Tehiat Yisrael* (Revival of Israel), *Petah Tikvah* (Door of Hope), and *Rosh Pinah* (Cornerstone), *Zion* and *Rishon le-Zion* (First of Zion), *Ezra ve* (and) *Nehemiah, Yesod Ha-maaleh* (Beginning of the Homecoming), and *Halutze Yesod Ha-maaleh* (Pioneers of the Homecoming—Ezra 7:9).

The names of the settlements and the organizations were symbolic and expressed the true nature of the "resettlement of Israel in its own land" inherent in them. In these names, as in the entire movement that began to stream toward Israel, were embodied the historical, national, and political aims of *Aliyah* (immigration) to Israel. This was understood by the immigrants, by the Jews generally, by the Turks and Arabs. The immigration was infused with a recognition of historical continuity, a recognition which grew gradually more intense as the resettlement progressed. *Eretz Yisrael* (the Land of Israel) was without unified administration, being divided by the Turks into a number of districts (Damascus, Beirut, and Jerusalem); and its Jewish population had already begun to send its children abroad because there was no possibility of economic sustenance for them at home. Yet unity of purpose in Jewish immigration and resettlement was achieved only through the power of recognition of Jewish historical destiny and the will of *all the Jewish people.*

This was clear to the Turks and Arabs. The Turkish government forbade entry into Israel, and from the 1880's until World War I its attitude was apparent: namely, to oppose the immigration and settlement of Jews there. Turkey claimed complete readiness to encourage Jewish settlement in any of her regions except Israel, and did all in her power to impede the development of the *Yishuv.* Rauf-al-Rauf, the Turkish governor of Jerusalem, was a bitter opponent of Jewish resettlement because he detected in it the vigor of a people resettling in its homeland, and he was tireless in his persistent efforts to mobilize in opposition both the Turkish government and the Arab populace.

The Jewish resettlement, unrelated to the demands of local conditions, and opposed by the government, necessitated extraordinary efforts, perseverance, efficiency, and administrative skill. It was infused with energy stemming from every segment of the Jewish people, from every historical factor of past generations. The settlers themselves were from different places: Hungary (*Petah Tikvah*), Russia (*Rishon le-Zion*), Lithuania (*Ekron*), Poland (*Yesod Ha-maaleh*), Romania (*Rosh Pinah* and *Zichron Yaakov* [Memorial to Jacob]) and Bulgaria (*Hartov* [Good Mountain]). And Jews from the entire Diaspora took an interest in the settlers' fortunes and supported them. To illustrate: Sigmund Zimmel, a Jew from Berlin who was a devoted adherent of the Lovers of Zion movement in Russia, went to Baron Rothschild to enlist his help for settlements in Upper Galilee (*Yesod Ha-maaleh* and *Rosh Pinah*) which had been founded by Jews from Poland and Romania. The Baron said: "Aren't you impressed by the remarkable fact that a Prussian Jew comes at the request of Russian Jews to a Parisian Jew to enlist his aid for Romanian and Polish Jews living in Israel?"

Indeed, the entire resettlement was accompanied by and dependent upon the combined endeavor of all Jews, as well as their organizational, financial, and political efforts. Neither the means nor the methods are of importance in this context. It is, however, a fact that Jewish lawyers of Spanish descent who had lived in Turkey and in Asia Minor and settled in Israel purchased land there with moneys acquired from Jews of Russia, Lithuania, Romania, and other countries, together with funds from Baron Rothschild and Baron de Hirsch (from the Jewish Colonization Organization) and others, and acquired title in the names of Jews who were citizens of Germany, France, England, and Turkey. It is again a fact that the interventions with the Turkish government on behalf of Jewish resettlement were based on the possibilities and realities of general Jewish life at that time: leaders of *Alliance Israélite Universelle*, rabbis and lay leaders, lawyers from Russia (Rosenfeld, Kalmanovitz), a member of the British Parliament (Montagu), an ambassador from the United States (Oscar S. Straus), a professor from Hungary (Arminius Vambery), and many others. The associations and organizations which preached Jewish emigration, which collected money for resettlement, and which were preoccupied with its problems, derived their organizational structures and methods of operation from Jewish groups in every part of the world, from charitable and mutual aid organizations, from corporate groups, *Haskalah* groups, youth groups, clandestine societies, fraternities, and revolutionary societies. The general Jewish reality also is indicated in the names of the organizations for land acquisition: for example, *Menuhah Ve-Nahala, Dorshei Zion, Agudath ha-Elef,* up to the various *ahuzot* (estates) and the setting up of urban *Shekunot* (quarters) in the cities of *Eretz Israel.* In other words, the actual establishment and crystallization of the *Yishuv* were made possible by the nature of the process of which it was the result.

III

This fact is customarily expressed in somewhat simpler terms: the fact is constantly stressed that the land was one to which people "went up" (*Aliyah*), not one to which people merely immigrated, and it was particularly this concept which enabled the builders of the *Yishuv* to achieve and carry the responsibility of independence.

To be sure, among the motives for *Aliyah* were also common factors which forced great masses of Jews to abandon the lands of their abode and to seek for themselves a new "birthplace"—such factors as the pogroms in Russia, the persecutions in Romania, the anti-Semitism in Germany, Austria, and western Europe, and others. But

174

of greater significance was the fact that decisive in the choice of Israel as the place for Jewish settlement was the longing for a resettlement of Israel in its own land.

During this period there were successive waves of immigration, and in every wave there was a substantial core of immigrants that had always felt themselves to be inhabitants of the Land of Israel. These men and women longed for a truly Jewish community, striving for and living a completely Hebrew cultural life. This desire to be a people dwelling in its own land, a people working its own earth, comprising the majority of the land's citizens and its constructive labor, gave direction and purpose to their immigration. These men and women knew the country well, though their knowledge came from the tradition, from literature, from legend; they recognized and remembered the names of its rivers and streams, hills and valleys, cities and villages. Before they emigrated, many had a clearer picture of the ways and paths of the land and the streets of Jerusalem than of the ways and cities of the countries in which they were born. In other words, *Aliyah* implies that these settlers carried within themselves both the Jewish community and the Jewish State, even while in the Diaspora.

Of no lesser importance was the fact that the *Aliyah* by its very nature brought to the land a vision of a new kind of Jew. Each of the immigration waves was composed of volunteers going to the aid of the Jewish people, of pioneers imbued with profound, collective, national feelings toward future tribulations. Each immigration wave was, therefore, a clarion call to young and fresh talents, who by their longing to build a path into the future were transformed from individuals into a mass movement. Thus every immigration wave eventually expressed a readiness for sacrifice, for acceptance of the yoke of responsibility for the future. And all of this with due consideration for the present, prompt reaction to developing events, and a vision of the distant future. All these are the basic factors in the creation of a society, any society.

Every wave of immigration brought those who knew Israel well, although neither they nor generations before them had trod upon it. Not an ordinary geographical area, but *The* Land, the Promised Land of the dream and the vision, of legends and miracles, of glory and splendor. To be sure, the immigrants encountered miserable living conditions. But while they were fully aware of the hardships of daily life, they were never reconciled to them. The present was not accepted as permanent fact, as a necessary condition of affairs, but was regarded as temporary, a transient reality, which the *Aliyah* would dissipate. The essential meaning of every *Aliyah* was the transformation of existing factors and the building of new factors conforming to *Aliyah* and to the spiritual nature of the immigrant. With this inner strength the *Aliyah* built the *Yishuv* and laid the foundations for a "fledgling state."

It is only through such an understanding of the situation that it is possible to comprehend the way the new Jewish community was formed. This extreme contradiction between the spiritual nature of the *Aliyah* and the reality naturally created an inner tension which by its very nature could not long endure. At first the entire *Aliyah* considered itself one unit, and the individual identified himself with the general, total undertaking, his very personality fluctuating with every forward or backward step in the building of the land, as though it were his own personal, intimate concern. However, eventually as a result of numbing tension, of wearying tumult, and of a fatigue which finally possessed a whole generation, individuals came naturally to identify the undertaking with themselves. After ten to fifteen harassing years, the members of each *Aliyah* began to regard themselves as the core of the entire undertaking, and measured its progress by the degree to which they themselves had achieved a firm foundation in the land.

This phenomenon was an established part of every *Aliyah*, but the reverses were always followed by advances. The *Yishuv* was constantly refreshed through the successive waves of immigration. New stirrings of the Exile resulting from echoes of disaster spread throughout the Diaspora, launching new waves of immigration and further building and pioneering, readiness for sacrifice, yearning for the homeland, agitation for a firm rooting there, and a sense of mission. These factors strengthened the efforts to create a new society. They built settlements, formed groups, united divergent feelings; and, because the tension never abated, the conditions necessary for the upbuilding of Israel served also to knit together the different parts of the Jewish people which, under other conditions, could never have been united. And so with *Aliyah* after *Aliyah* and layer after layer, the new Jewish settlement gradually developed, a settlement of the people dwelling in Zion. This was the great historic mission of the second *Aliyah*, the third *Aliyah*, and every subsequent *Aliyah*. Every wave of immigration brought fine building blocks and elements which acted as magnets, drawing toward themselves the basic elements of previous waves. In this way the various social bases for the independence of Israel were steadily enlarged.

IV

Both the immigration waves and the "self-mobilization" of the Jewish "social factors" in aid of resettlement testify to the existence of resources within the people which, by their nature, served as an impetus for action; these resources were as if destined to bring about Jewish resettlement in the homeland. To be sure, the immigration waves were limited in scope and the interwining of the "Jewish social factors" with the progress of the resettlement was extremely slow; it was only by degrees that broader sections of the "Jewish world" were joined to this development.

But, on the other hand, already revealed in the early history of the Lovers of Zion movement—easily understood as the "rebellion against the Exile"—was a power to penetrate all the widespread segments of the Jewish people, a persistence and continuity of action, and a stubborn clinging to past accomplishments. These traits testified to a profound reawakening of a people, in which were renewed and revealed such primary and essential factors as land, language, and social cohesion.

Even before the actual resettlement, a desire for the covenant with the land was renewed in the hearts of the people—not only because this covenant already existed but because it was (as stated above) a basic factor in Jewish life.

Many are inclined to claim that, in part, this "covenant"

was not significant, not a fundamental frame of reference, and not something basic to present reality. Everywhere Jews prayed for "dew and rain," for "wind and rains"—in conformity with the climate of Israel—ate of the fruit of the land on the fifteenth of *Shevat*, and made Jerusalem the focus of all their joyous and mournful holidays. Yet some state that this "covenant" was merely an intense, imaginary longing tied to dreams of Redemption, to a vision of the future: beyond actual attainment, at most a matter of the spirit, with no temporal foundation in the land itself.

But this concept overlooks the significant historic fact that the desire for resettlement was strong throughout the generations, that the struggle for the establishment and maintenance of the *Yishuv* continued through all the generations, and that at all times and from all Jewish communities those groups that included a maximum of Jewish living had streamed to Israel. The extreme elements— those who would not come to terms with the Exile, those who tried to hasten the day of decision—were attracted to the Holy Land, "to stand" (as one living in the ninth century put it) in the gate, because "if they seek mercy, it is incumbent upon those who incurred the anger to stand at the gates of the palace of the King who was angry at His sons, therefore they go to His home to seek mercy." The age-old *Yishuv* in its persistent clinging to the land was objectively and partly consciously the emissary of the people destined to prepare the way for Redemption. This was true of the eighth and ninth centuries, of the time of the Mourners of Zion, and of the messianic movements; also of the time of Jehudah Halevi, Maimonides, and Nahmanides; of the emigration from Germany at the end of the thirteenth century; and of the expulsion from Spain, the emigration to Safed, and the immigration of the extremely pious and ascetic Jews (*Hassidim* and *Perushim*) at the end of the eighteenth and beginning of the nineteenth century; and this was true also of the immigration of the devout Jews and the pupils of Hatham Sofer from Hungary. The whole concept was expressed by a *Haskalah* poet, Adam Hakohen, in his poem about the old *Yishuv*, written approximately 110 years ago.

It should also be noted that the Land of Israel and the settlement there was a magnetic attraction, and not only from an abstract point of view. The *Yishuv* continually sent forth messengers, preachers, and propagandists, who fanned the flame and who may be considered, as it were, the "guardians of the covenant" with the land, from the time of the messengers of Zion up to the eighteenth and nineteenth centuries and the later voices crying out for *Aliyah* until today. There was also an entire literature, with unique characteristics and motifs, which testifies to this love of Zion and Jerusalem. It is sufficient to mention the letters from those living in Israel to those in the Exile which, from the nineteenth century until the present day, filled the Jewish press (both that published in Hebrew and that published in other languages) with word which upheld and strengthened the living tie with the land.

Who responded? Those who because of their social status were moved to emigrate, those who had been reared most thoroughly in the Jewish tradition; and these characteristics were frequently combined.

"Exile" and "Redemption" are not merely abstract ideological concepts which varied from generation to generation with changes in the outlook and understanding, in the beliefs and opinions, of Jews. "Exile" and "Redemption" are systems of concepts and social perceptions which absorb the experience of generations, the experience of the misfortunes of Exile and the trials of Redemptions. All of traditional, mystical Jewish thought is suffused with these historical experiences. Those elements of the people (not many, to be sure) which were moved by this tradition of constant search for ways of Redemption, fulfillment, and spiritual activity were always ready to go to the Land of Israel.

This was true also of later generations. Not only from the ranks of the messianic movements, from the various off-shoots of Sabbateanism which constantly stimulated the search for ways of Redemption, but also from the ranks of Hassidism and the followers of Elijah Gaon, and others, came those who spurred the return to Israel. Their immigration was dependent upon varying ideologies, but the common factor was the longing for a way of life in which the boundaries between the sacred and the profane would be dissolved through the sanctification of the profane. For all such immigrants the Land of Israel was an anteroom where the Jew could prepare himself for his lofty destiny. This historic element acted as a causative factor in moulding the *Yishuv*. The *Aliyah* to the Land of Israel was regarded by every immigrant not merely as a geographical change but as a further step toward the attainment of human perfection.

V

The period of the *Haskalah* and the Emancipation apparently uprooted the Jew from the world of the past. The slogan of the *Haskalah* was, "Be aware of your time and your place," and the aim of the Emancipation was to infuse a sense of permanence and stability in the land of the Jew's birth. One well-known nineteenth-century German Jew expressed this in a uniquely grotesque manner in his address on the Ninth Day of Av when he urged gratitude for the destruction of the Temple and the subsequent Exile because, as a result, he and others of his generation were privileged to be subjects of the Prussian king. However, not all Jews shared this feeling. We can easily believe the testimony of another member of that German generation who complained that he was constantly receiving letters from young Jews concerning news from Israel and the immigration of Jews, all of the letters filled with justifiable yearnings "to find at least a tiny spot on earth where one can feel himself completely free." The existence of this feeling and its enduring influence was one of the causes of the bitter polemics of some groups of German Reform Jews who sought to alter, or, to be accurate, to restrict the emphasis on the Land of Israel in the Jewish religion.

The Hebrew language, its vitality and scope, were far stronger and more deeply rooted than is customarily assumed, even during the period when linguistic identification was thought necessary for the political, legal, and social equality of Jews in the Diaspora. And even in that period, though suffering a staggering cultural and linguistic decline, on the one hand, and severe restrictions upon their Jewish creativity, on the other, a segment of the Jews nurtured longings for full Jewish cultural, political, and social independence.

The tension between those who furthered Hebrew and those who furthered other studies is illustrated by Mendele Moicher Sforim (pen name of Shalom Jacob Abramowitsch). At first glance, Mendele's introduction to his story "My Old Mare," and the story concerning "the Jewish boy who lost his sanity as a result of examinations in Russian literature," appear to be critical of those Russian educational techniques and standards which permitted the expression in ridiculous terms of the legends and early poetry of Russia. But actually from an experimental viewpoint Mendele is showing the psychological rebellion of the Jewish youth who, against his will, was taken from his own spiritual world to an entirely new world. One hundred and ten years ago there existed in Odessa a school, under the guidance of the *Maskil* Bezalel Stern, in which modern Hebrew literature was studied. Among the teachers was Simha Pinsker, and among the subjects were the writings of Samuel David Luzzatto, Isaac Baer Levenson, and the like, along with those of the newer Hebrew poets. In private correspondence and correspondence found in newspapers from the 1850's and 1860's, there is ample testimony to the way education was deprived of modern Hebrew elements and the distress this caused in the hearts of individuals, many echoes being preserved in Jewish literature.

The elegy of Isaac Eichal on the decline of the Hebrew language in Germany, *The History of the Pioneer* by Isaac Erter with his dreams of the revival of Hebrew, and the dirge of J. L. Gordon in his poem "For Whom Do I Labor?", expressed the sadness of those who constantly experienced the "covenant of the generations" both culturally and traditionally, and whose souls at the same time yearned for a completely new way of life. Also in this circle there arose the individual immigrants who gave new form and quality to the reestablishment of Israel.

It is no acident that the immigration in the 1890's and

at the turn of the century was from Russia, at a time when Russian literature and Russian Jewish schools exerted pressure upon Jewish education, even in the townlets of the Pale of Settlement. The novel *Against the Stream* by Isaiah Bershadski gives only a meager picture of this background. The influence of the Emancipation was not limited to those localities where Jews enjoyed equality, but was also felt where Jews had not as yet achieved legal and civil rights. Even in those countries Jews participated in the struggle for general cultural and political freedom, and to that extent participated in the general life of the state and its society. If Moses Hess was the first Jew in the West who sensed the restrictions placed by the realities of the Exile upon the social creativity of the Jewish group, thousands and tens of thousands sensed it in the East. Paradoxically, the effort to rebuild society generally and the depth of the current social ferment made many Jews aware of the Jewish reality for the first time, and stirred them to readiness for future events.

VI

But perhaps the most significant factor in the rebirth of Israel was the independent nature which characterized the new settlement. Independence is never achieved save through independence. Historical experience taught the Jews that it was impossible to maintain inner independence unless their inner lives were free. The words of Hillel, "If I be not for myself who shall be for me?" which Pinsker proclaimed as a slogan of the Love of Zion movement, contained profound political wisdom, and were not only a theoretical truth but also a fundamental guiding force in all the endeavors to which the Zionist movement was dedicated. The high Turkish official, Rauf-al-Rauf, expressed his opposition to the Jewish resettlement: "The Jews enter the land, acquire properties, build settlements, establish schools, all as though there were no Turkish government, as though the land were already in their possession. Is there really no need," he queried, "to ask us, to have us join their program? Has the Land of Israel already been taken from us and given to the Jews?" Rauf-al-Rauf understood the true political significance of the Jewish efforts far better than did the Jewish statesmen and savants who mocked the attempts of the Lovers of Zion to nullify the political *status quo*.

This independence was prevalent in the *Aliyah*, in the resettlement, and in the *Haganah*; and to all these the past experiences of Jewish life were applied. To the area of economic life the Jews in Israel transferred all the experience acquired in the countries where they had lived. From the very beginning of the resettlement they established their own self-government; set up councils and executive committees, land registries, courts of law, and ordinances; founded kindergartens, elementary schools, high schools; and opened schools of education and higher learning. All of this they accomplished by themselves.

Out of inner deliberations and discussions and without any interference on the part of government, they utilized both their individual and collective experience, and thereby constantly renewed their social creativity, which for the first time was being given opportunity for full expression and implementation.

185

This was plain with the *Haganah*. The people did not rely solely on the government for security, but learned to fall back on their own experience and utilized that of Jewish soldiers who had served in the armies of various countries and in various wars—the Franco-Prussian War, the Russo-Turkish War, the Russo-Japanese War, the First World War, the Russian Civil War, and the revolutionary underground. In this way they established means for their own protection, in this way the *Shomer* (the Jewish Militia) was organized, and in this way—from their own experiences—the *Haganah*, a national underground army, was made up of tens of thousands of disciplined volunteers. In this way factories and war industries were established underground. In this way an "illegal" navy was created which transported "illegal" immigrants, and a system of secret air transit was organized to bring additional immigrants. Jews who had fought in the Second World War and the Allied Armies, with the United States Air Force, in Britain, North Africa, and so on, took part in all these efforts. And all around them widespread segments of the people mobilized and grouped together—particularly after the destruction of European Jewry.

To sum up: the political rebirth of Israel is the very essence of Jewish history. She absorbed into herself the experiences and activities of generations, the covenant of generations. She renewed the covenant with the land out of a longing, through the creation of a new community, to develop the Covenant of Man into an Eternal Covenant.

BOOK ONE
Israel in Diaspora

1. Cf. Caussent, *Les dispersés d'Israël* (Paris, 1929), pp. 12–16.

2. R. Bahai the son of R. Asher, in his commentary to the Pentateuch, at the end of the portion *Lech Lecha*.

3. *Ha-Cuzari*, II, 24

4. Cf. *Ketubot*, 111a, and the commentary of Rashi.

5. Cf. my article "Diaspora Communities and Their Destruction," *Knesset* (1944), 47–52, in Hebrew, on the spread of the Dispersion and the numbers of the Jews in it.

6. In his lecture published in the Russian quarterly *Jewzey-skaja Stazina* (1910), p. 156.

7. Introduction to Pt. V (German ed. 1871), pp. xv and xvii.

8. Saadiah Gaon, *Emunoth we-Deoth* (Leipzig, 1859), Chap. III, p. 80.

9. Jost, *Geschichte d. Israeliten*. In his great History (Pt. XI, pp. 454–457), Graetz took Jost to task for in fact following a Christian historian of the beginning of the eighteenth cent., Jacob Basnage (who, in his *L'Histoire des Juifs*, I-VII, Rotterdam, 1707–1711, also gave an account of Jewish history by Diaspora communities), and for "persisting in his errors in his old age too." The injustice of this stricture will undoubtedly be evident to anyone who makes a careful study of Jost's general views. These are based on an entirely independent conception of the course of Jewish history, which, when measured by the state of scientific research in his day, can only

187

evoke our admiration. Many of Jost's opinions and theories have been revived in a modernized form and in several respects deserve a hearing even today. For a candid, generally just, and basically correct estimation of Jost's work, see Bernfeld's excellent article "Dorshei Reshumot," *Hashiloah*, Vol. II, pp. 203–208.

10. Jost, Pt. V, p. 226; p. 16. Jost's remarks are, in part, directed against the view expressed by Solomon Lewisohn in his article, "The condition of the Jews in the Berber lands, with some historical notes on the beginning of their settlement there down to modern times," *Schulamit*, Vol. IV, Pt. I, No. 4, p. 528. Lewisohn maintained that in the Orient there was no "concentrated, nationally conscious Jewish population capable of acting in concert," otherwise "the heroic rebelliousness (of the Jews), which is unequalled in the historical records of all other nations, would certainly have speedily restored to the world its freedom and to the nations their national rights." Lewisohn subsequently included this article in his small but valuable book *Vorlesungen über neuere jüd. Geschichte* (Vienna, 1820). The last sentence is omitted in the book.

11. Jost, *op. cit.*, Pt. V, p. 11.

12. Jost's four historiographical works are:
    1) *Geschichte d. Israeliten seit d. Zeit der Maccabäer bis auf unsere Tage* (1820–1828), in 9 parts.
    2) *Allg. Geschichte d. Israelit. Volkes* (1831–1832), in 2 vols.
    3) *Neuere Geschichte d. Israeliten in der erste Hälfte d. XIX Jahrhunderts*, I–III (1846–1847).
    4) *Geschichte d. Judenthums u. seiner Sekten*, I–III (1857–1859).

13. This is the method that Jost himself actually tried, for the most part, to follow in his historical writing.

14. Thus, for example, even Selig (Paulus) Cassel shows the

influence of Jost, in his article *"Juden (Geschichte)"* in Vol. 27 of the *Ersch-Gruber General Encyclopedia*, pp. 1–238. In this article—published in 1850 and still of value today—which deals with the "period from the destruction of the Temple by Titus in 70 C.E. to modern times," Cassel divides the world history *(Weltgeschichte)* of the Jews into three parts: (1) the history of the Jews in the Roman Empire; (2) the history of the social and political status of the Jews in Christian Europe; and (3) the history of the Jews in the ("Mohammedan") areas ruled by Islam and in lands outside Europe.

15. P. 3 (in the 2nd edition, 1866).

16. P. xv (published in 1871).

17. *Ibid.*

18. *Ibid.*

19. *Ibid.*, p. xviii.

20. *Ibid.*, pp. xviii–xix.

21. *Ibid.*, Pt. IV, p. 4.

22. *Ibid.*, p. 3.

23. In Graetz's magnum opus, the eight volumes dealing with Jewish history from the destruction of the Second Temple to the middle of the nineteenth century are divided as follows: Vol. IV—from the loss of Jewish statehood to the final completion of the Talmud; Vol. V—from the final completion of the Talmud to the flowering of Spanish-Jewish culture (1027); Vol. VI— from the flowering of Spanish-Jewish culture to the death of Maimonides (1205); Vols. VII and VIII— from the death of Maimonides to the expulsion of the Jews from Spain and Portugal; Vol. IX—from the expulsion from Spain and Portugal to the permanent settlement of the Marranos in Holland (1618); Vol. X

—from the settlement of the Marranos in Holland to the beginning of the Mendelssohnian period (1750); Vol. XI—from the beginning of the Mendelssohnian period to modern times (1848).

24. Cf., Graetz, Pt. IV, p. 1, and also the Introduction to Pt. V, pp. xiv–xvi.

25. Cf., Graetz, Pt. V, p. xv.

26. Graetz regarded Palestine as the bond connecting the Torah, on the one hand, with the hope of redemption and the belief in the coming of the Messiah, on the other. Cf., Graetz, IV, p. 4.

27. "The body and soul of Judaism," in Graetz's expression. *Op. cit.* Pt. V, p. xiv.

28. Cf., the article by David Kaufmann on Graetz, *Gesammetle Schriften*, I, pp. 272–282; and also Meisel's book on Graetz, *Heinrich Graetz* (1917), pp. 34–70.

29. Dubnow remarks, in his above-mentioned work (p. 156), that the conception of Jewish history as the history of Judaism arose at the time of the Reform movement in western Europe and through its influence. There is certainly some truth in this observation (and not only in relation to Graetz's views). But account must also be taken of the history of Jewish thought as a whole, and above all of the influence of Krochmal and his school.

30. *Wissenschaftliche Zeitschrift für jüdische Theologie*, Vol. I (1835), p. 180.

31. Cf., Geiger, "The General Introduction to the Science of Judaism," *Nachgelassene Schriften*, Vol. II, pp. 62–65. Cf., Also, Ellbogen, in the collection of articles, *Abraham Geiger* (1910), p. 331.

32. Cf., Geiger, *op. cit.*, p. 61.

33. Cf., *Ibid.*, pp. 63–64.

34. In the second edition (Breslau, 1910), pp. 168–169. Cf., *ibid.*, pp. 152–156, 167–172, 361–381.

35. In Russian "Tchto Takoe *Jewzeyskaja Jstoija?*" published in the monthly, *Woshod* (1893), Bks. X–XI, pp. 111–142 and Bk. XII, pp. 78–112. Translated into German by Israel Friedlander: *Die jüdische Geschichte, ein geschichtsphilosophischer Versuch* (Berlin, 1897, Frankfurt a/M, 1921); and into English: *Jewish History, an Essay in the Philosophy of History* (1903).

36. *Woshod* (1893), Bks. X–XI, pp. 118–120.

37. *Ibid.*

38. Cf. *Ibid.*, pp. 126–127. Dubnow designates the nineteenth century as the period of European enlightenment for Jewry as a whole, without singling out any particular Jewish community as the center. The place of the weakened religious awareness was now taken by a newly emerging historical consciousness composed of physical, intellectual and moral elements, of habits, philosophical views (particularly the belief in absolute monotheism), emotions and feelings which had become part of the Jewish heritage down the generations. But what Dubnow here calls "historical consciousness" is in fact simply the Jewish awareness of being a nation and, as such, was certainly not a product solely of the nineteenth century. It *created* the science of Jewish history in that century, and was not created by it.

39. *Ibid.*, p. 119.

40. Cf., his article in *Jewzeyskaja Stazina* (1910), p. 157. Subsequently, in the preface to his *History of the Jewish People*, Pt. I, pp. 1–13, Dubnow formulated these views of his in more general terms, but without changing their essential content. Cf. *History of the Jewish People*, Pt. I, p. 7, note.

41. *Ibid.*, p. 156.

42. *Ibid.* Cf. also his *Divrei Yimei Am Olam*, Pt. I, pp. 8–9.

43. Ibid., p. 156.

44. Cf., my remarks on Pt. VII or his great work (in German) in *Kiryath Sefer*, Year 6, pp. 219–221 (in Hebrew).

45. *Ibid.* Dubnow was, of course, aware of these shortcomings inherent in his method, and even explained his reasons for his arrangement of the material, on the assumption that in this way the numerous difficulties could be circumvented. For a further estimation of Dubnow's work cf. my article "Simon Dubnow and His Historiographical Achievement," in the *Davar Year Book* for 1950–51, pp. 317–325 (in Hebrew).

46. Täubler propounded his views in the first and third numbers of the *Mitteilungen d. Gesamtarchivs d. deutschen Juden* (Berlin, 1908, 1912); in the 31st report (for the year 1912) of the *Lehranstalt f.d. Wissenschaft d. Judenthums* (Berlin 1913); and in the still unpublished lectures given by him in the Higher Institute of Jewish Learning where the present writer had the good fortune to be his pupil.

47. 31st *Bericht d. Lehranstalt f.d. Wissenschaft d. Judenthums*, p. 50.

48. *Mitteilungen d. Gesamtarchivs d. deutschen Juden*, I, 1908, pp. 2–3.

49. *Ibid.*

50. *Op. cit.*, No. 3, 1921, pp. 64–74. It is true that Täubler propounded these views of his only in connection with the principles to be observed in the division of the historical material preserved in the archives. But the principal innovations in his method—the recognition of the true nature of "the process of struggle" and the deter-

mining of the relation between general and Jewish history—are important and valid for the whole of Jewish history in the Diaspora.

51. Cf., my book *Israel in Its Land* (in Hebrew), Pt. I, p. 96, and paragraph IV, note 4.

52. The general historical significance of the tens of different names by which the Jewish people referred to itself calls for a special study of its own. The present writer has touched on the subject in two lectures, one on "The Character of the Jewish Nation in the Historical Consciousness of the Jewish People," and the other on "The Jewish People's Evidence About Itself, and Its Value as a Source of Historical Information."

53. On the periods of "stability" and "crisis" in the various parts of the Diaspora cf. my article "Diaspora Communities and Their Destruction" (in Hebrew, *Knesset*, 8, 1944), pp. 46–60.

54. There was a very steep decline in the influence of Germany after the persecutions in the 14th century (during the "Black Death" and even prior to it), of Spain in the fifteenth century (after the anti-Jewish decrees of 1391), and of Poland in the second half of the seventeenth and in the eighteenth century (after the Chiemelnicki massacres). In every one of these countries the crisis was of such great proportions as to reduce the Jewish community virtually to a state of paralysis in which it could no longer continue to exercise its previous influence.

55. Summarized from my lecture on "The History of the *Yishuv* and Its Place in General Jewish History as a Historiographical Problem," which was published in *Collected Articles on Jewish Studies* (in Hebrew), pp. 371–377.

56. On the character of the two last periods, cf. my book *Crossroads* (in Hebrew, Bialik Foundation, 1956), pp. 68–69.

57. On this matter cf. "Ben Yehuda and the Revival of the Hebrew Language" in my book *Trail-Blazers* (in Hebrew, Tel Aviv, 1946), pp. 5–20; and also *Crossroads, op. cit.*, pp. 248–251.

BOOK TWO
The Modern Period

1. Cf., *Cambridge Modern History*, I, pp. 1–2, in Grayton's introductory note.

2. Cf., e.g., Graetz in his preface to Vol. XI of his great work, and also at the beginning of chap. 1 of the same volume. Cf., also Dubnow, *Weltgeschichte d. jüd. Volkes*, Pt. I, pp. 44–52 (in chap. 2 of the introduction devoted to "The Main Points in the Historical Developments of Recent Times").

3. Cf., Graetz, Vol. IV, pp. 1–6 (written in 1866); Dubnow, *Weltgeschichte*, Vol. I, Introduction B.

4. Of the twelve chapters in Vol. IX of Graetz's work, which deals with Jewish history in the years 1750–1848, three are devoted to the *Haskalah* movement and its consequences (Mendelssohn, the literary journals, the "salons," the Science of Judaism, and religious reforms); three to *Hassidism*, the French Revolution, and the Damascus blood libel; and three others to the interrelation between events in the non-Jewish world and inner developments in Jewry. In contrast to this, in the three parts of Dubnow's work dealing with the period from the French Revolution to the First World War (1789–1914), only 40 of the 157 sections are given to domestic Jewish problems (the spiritual trends in Judaism, religious reforms, the Science of Judaism, the nationalist-Zionist movement, etc.). Three quarters of the whole work are devoted to an account of the position of the

Jews in the gentile world, principally from the legal and political standpoint.

5. Actually, I. M. Yost (*Geschichte der Israeliten*, IX, 7, 18, 28) had already singled out the year 1740 as the beginning of "modern Jewish history in Christian Europe"—the period of "spiritual liberation, the decline of the rabbinate, the appearance of civic freedom, and the spread of science." Jost, however, associated the beginning of this period with the personality of Frederick II, who, for Jost, was the symbol of the "modern era." Graetz's view was accepted by all subsequent Jewish historians.

6. Martin Philippsohn, *Neueste Geschichte des jüdischen Volkes* (1907), was the first to begin modern Jewish history with the "dawn of freedom" and the French Revolution, and not with the *Haskalah* movement.

7. Cf., Graetz, Vol. XI, p. 3.

8. Cf., *ibid.*, p. 1: "The fourth period in Jewish history, the period of growing self-recognition. The first phase, the phase of ferment and struggle."

9. Cf., *ibid.*, Introduction to Vol. XI.

10. Cf., Dubnow, *Weltgeschichte*, Pt. I, pp. 44–50.

11. Cf., e.g., S. Baron, *A Social and Religious History of the Jews* (1937), II, pp. 164–165.

12. In rabbinical literature (homiletical works and responsa) and in popular writings (books of moral instruction and the like), and also in collections of Jewish memoirs, there is abundant evidence of the following "social phenomena" in the communities of western Europe: lack of reverence for the Torah and disregard of the authority of the rabbinate; disregard of Sabbath observance and general laxity in the performance of the *mitzvot*; changes in manners and ways of life as a result

of closer relations with the gentile world; a growth of sexual immorality; and an increase in the study of languages other than Hebrew.

13. Cf., the important material collected in Priebatsch, "Die Judenpolitik des fürstichlen Absolutismus im 17 und 18 Jahrhundert, Forschungen und Versuche . . . ," *Festschrift f. D. Schaefer*, pp. 561–641. Also Selma Stern's important work *The Court Jew* (Philadelphia, 1950), which presents the results of this scholar's researches into the rise and fate of the "Court Jew" and gives a very interesting description of his character, now regarded by the authoress as "a typical phenomenon representative of the general development of Jewish history" (Preface, p. XII). However, this latter work in fact deals only with the position of the "Court Jew" in the gentile state and in gentile society, without taking any account of the impact made by both his rise and fall on the world of the Jewish masses and the inner life of Jewry.

Generally speaking, it must be stated that there is no really definitive account of the way in which this upper stratum of Jews came to occupy important positions in the economy of the gentile state. The requisite material is to be found scattered about in separate monographs on different congregations, communities and families, or in biographies of leading Jewish figures.

14. This is presumably why Jewish scholars in eastern Europe regarded "modern" Jewish history as beginning not only with the personality of Mendelssohn and the *Haskalah* movement in western Europe, but also with the appearance of *Hassidism* and its leader, the Baal Shem Tob, in the Ukraine, and with the spiritual awakening in Lithuania inspired by the Gaon of Vilna. Mendelssohn, the Baal Shem, and the Vilna Gaon were the "three shepherds" who were charged with strengthening the three pillars of Judaism. "The Study of the

Torah, Faith, and Enlightenment," *Kiryah Neemanah*, p. 142.

15. Cf., John Toland, *Reasons for Naturalizing the Jews in Great Britain* (1714).

16. Cf., *Tarbiz* (in Hebrew), Vol. VIII, p. 89.

17. Wilhelm Surenhuys. Cf., Graetz, Vol. X, pp. 312–314, and pp. 287–289.

18. Basnage, in the Introduction to Vol. III of his *L'Histoire et la religion des Juifs depuis Jésus-Christ jusqu'à present* (1706–1711). Cf., Graetz, *ibid.*, pp. 315–317.

19. Cf., Eisenmenger, *Entdecktes Judenthum*, Vol. II (1711), pp. 997, 1015, 1023; and Hartmann, *Eisenmenger und seine jüdischen Gegner* (1834). Cf., *Jew. Enc.*, V, 80–82.

20. Cf., Kaufmann, *Aus Heinrich Heine's Ahnensaal* (1896), pp. 57–62.

21. Hayyiun, *Divrei Nehemiah* (Berlin, 1743), Portion of the Law *Behar*.

22. Besides the rabbis and sages who immigrated to Palestine from Islamic lands (European Turkey, Asia Minor and North Africa), there were also many who came from the congregations of Italy, Bohemia, Poland, and Lithuania. A complete list of such rabbinical immigrants in the eighteenth century would be very instructive historically.

23. Abundant material concerning the emissaries from Palestine and their influence on the congregations to which they were sent (especially in the Balkan countries, the Orient and Italy) is to be found in the responsa of contemporary rabbis. Cf., Yaari, *Sheluhei Eretz Yisrael* (Jerusalem, 1951).

24. *Torat Hakannaut*, Lwow edition (1860), p. 58.

25. P. Beer, *Lehren und Meinungen aller bestandenen und noch bestehenden religiösen Sekten der Juden . . .* (1822–23), II, 297. Beer's information about the vicissitudes of the Shabbathian emissaries may be of historical value, since he himself was a native of Bohemia and perhaps also close to the circles in question. Cf., G. Shalom, "Information About the Followers of Sabbatai Zevi in the Works of Missionaries in the 18th Century" (in Hebrew), *Zion* (Year 9), pp. 27–38, 84–88.

26. Cf., Shalom, *op. cit.*, pp. 86–88.

27. Almost all the laws concerning the Jews in the states of central and western Germany in the eighteenth century deal with the problem of "foreign Jews" and show the concern of the authorities about the increase in the number of Jews in the state as a result of this migratory movement. Cf., e.g., with regard to Prussia: Selma Stern, *Der preussische Staat und die Juden*, I, 2 (1925), documents 454, 457 (1702), 466, 474 (1705), 496 (1708), 501 (1709), 507, 508 (1710), 521, 524, 525 (1712); I. Freund, *Die Emanzipation der Juden in Preussen*, 1912, II, 10 (the Charter of 1714, clause 15), 18 (the Charter of 1730, clause 10), 42–44 (clauses XX–XXIII of the General Charter of 1750); with regard to Austria, and especially the congregation of Vienna, cf., Pribram, *Urkunden und Akten Zur Geschichte der Juden in Wien*, 1918, I, 126 (1707), 136 (1717), 144 (1725), 156 (1747), 161 (clauses 25–29; 1753), 179 (clauses 6, 16–20, 28; from the year 1762), 179 (1764); Josef II's Edict of Toleration (205, XVI, clause 20); 218 (from the year 1783; the Jews' freedom of migratory movement from Bohemia and Galicia to Hungary); 227 (1788). For France, cf., sections a–e in the Lettres Patentes of Louis XVI from the year 1784 (Lucien-Brun, *La condition des Juifs en France depuis 1789*, pp. 317–318). Cf., also the concern of Michaelis about the influx of "wan-

dering Jews" (Dohen, *Über bürgerliche Verbesserung der Juden*, II, 1783, pp. 52–53).

28. Cf., Schudt, *Jüdische Merkwürdigkeiten*, II, with additions p. 59.

29. Cf., the famous speech of Clermont-Tonneur: Halphen, *Receuil des lois, décrets, ordonnances etc. concernant les Israélites* (1851), pp. 184–186; and the letter of Grégoire to Isaiah Bing, Graetz (German), Vol. XI, p. 202 (note).

30. Cf., e.g., the homilectical sermon of R. Yehezkel Landa on this matter (*Ahavat Zion*, sermon 3).

31. Geiger, in his letter to Dérenbourg, dated Nov. 22, 1840, published by Ludwig Geiger, *Allg. Zeitung d. Judenthums* (1896), No. 24, p. 284.

32. A detailed and thorough study of this question has still to be made. At all events, it is worth remarking that, as early as the middle of the eighteenth century, Lazarus (Eliezer) Ben-David, a native of Berlin, was, as a child, taught German before he knew Hebrew. Cf., his autobiographical sketch, re-published by Moritz Stern in the fifth number of *Beiträge zur Geschichte der Jüdischen Gemeinde zu Berlin* (1934), pp. 3–4.

33. The number of Jewish pupils in both general schools (secondary and primary grades) and Jewish schools who were taught in the language of the state rose from nearly 59,000 (in 1886) to more than 312,000 (in 1911). Of this latter number more than 200,000 attended schools founded by Jews. Cf. the *Russian-Jewish Encyclopedia*, Vol. XIII, pp. 57–58. In the years 1884–1893 alone, 232 such schools were opened by Jews.

34. Num. xxiii, 9.

35. In this connection, the exegetic and homiletic rabbinical literature right down to the most recent times contains

very valuable historical material which has not yet been fully exploited.

36. The stirring of Jewish self-awareness and of the sense of Jewish brotherhood in the wake of persecutions and anti-Jewish decrees was no less characteristic of modern times than of previous generations. It may also be argued that the "Science of Judaism" and modern Jewish self-recognition owed their origins to anti-Semitic utterances, such as, "Hep Hep." On the nature of the spontaneous Jewish reaction to those events see Alexander Weil's account of their effect on Joseph Salvador (*Allg. Zeitung d. Jud.*, 1839, No. 89, 90, pp. 472, 482). Similarly, the general Jewish awareness of the need for mutual assistance, which led to the founding of the *Kol Yisrael Haverim* association, was aroused by the Damascus blood libel and the Mortara affair (this is only hinted at by Narcisse Leven in *Fifty Years of History*, pp. 63–66).

37. Cf. Riesser, in the third chapter of *Vertheidigung der bürgerlichen Gleichstellung der Juden* (1831) which deals with the national aspect of the question (Riesser's *Collected Works*, Vol. II, pp. 129–159, and also the end of the article, pp. 183–184). Also, in his *Über die Stellung d. Bekenner d. Mosäischen Glaubens in Deutschland* (1831), see his remarks on the Jews' feeling of belonging to Germany, to its language, its literature and its culture, on their loyalty to that country's laws and their desire to be Germans (Pt. II, pp. 85–96). When Riesser emphasized that "we are not immigrants, but natives of the country" and that, precisely because "we are natives of the country, we have no claims on any other fatherland and are hence either Germans or homeless," he was undoubtedly expressing the attitude of the great majority of his contemporaries. It was this line of defense that won him the admiration and esteem of the German Jewish public, and also evoked a sympathetic

response from Germans who were not usually pro-Jewish.

38. The unifying nationalistic influence of the Jewish press has not been properly appreciated, much less satisfactorily investigated. A few facts will illustrate the importance of this matter. From 1837—the year of the appearance of the *Allgemeine Zeitung d. Judentums,* the first Jewish paper to have as one of its principal aims the publication of news about Jewish life in the various lands of the Diaspora—to 1881, the year of the great turning point in Jewish history, no fewer than 1,505 newspapers appeared in 20 countries and in sixteen languages. The range of the information provided by this Jewish press widened from year to year. Thus, for example, in its first year the *Allg. Z. d. J.* carried news about Jewish life from forty localities in the German states and from thirty-five in other countries. In its second year (1838) the paper already published reports from 85 localities in the German states and from sixty places in twenty countries outside Germany. In its tenth year (1846), the numbers were approximately 100 localities and districts in Germany, and 85 places in twenty-three other countries. In the sixtieth year (1896), every single issue of the paper, which now appeared once a week, carried reports and letters on Jewish affairs from scores of communities in Germany and other countries. The other papers that appeared at the same time—Jost's *Israelitische Annalen* (1839–1841), Fürst's *Orient* (1840–1851)—contained more of their own reporting (by their own special correspondents) than the *Allg. Z. d. J.* Among the regular contributors to all three of these papers were S. D. Luzzatto, Jost, Graetz and Yellinik, Holdheim and Formstacher, Alexander Weil (Paris) and Arnheim, M. A. Ginzburg and J. L. Gordon, Slonimski and R. Levi Hirsch Chajes, and many other important contemporary figures.

39. On the emigration from Germany to these countries cf., *Israelitische Annalen* (1839), pp. 213–214; (1840), pp. 73–74; *Allg. Zeitungd. Jud.* (1847), pp. 674, 731–733. Cf., Leschinski, *The Beginnings of Jewish Emigration & Colonization in the Nineteenth Century* (in Yiddish, Berlin, 1929), pp. 51–68. Cf. also Weinryb, *Deutsche-jüdische Wanderungen im 19 Jahrhundert, Morgen* (April 1934).

40. Some of the oldest and most distinguished families in the Sephardi congregations in London came from Italy, e.g., the Eliases, Meldolas, Montefiores, and Disraelis. Cf., Gaster, *History of the Ancient Synagogue* (1901), p. 125; and also *Jew. Encycl.*, VIII, pp. 450–459 (on the history of the Meldola family).

41. Particularly numerous were the Jews from North Africa (principally from Algiers and Tunis) who settled in the coastal towns of these countries (Leghorn, Marseilles, and others).

42. The emigration from Germany was particularly marked during the period of Prussian rule in Warsaw. The emigration of the "Lithuanians" to Poland was one of the most important of the "social phenomena" of Jewish life, particularly in Lodz and Warsaw, and influenced the industrial development there.

43. Cf., Schatzky, *Geschichte von Juden in Warschau*, I, (New York 1947), p. 1958. The emigration during the period of Prussian rule consisted mainly of wealthy families. Cf., the article by P. Friedmann, "Wirtschaftliche Umschichtungsprozesse und Industrialisierung in der polnischen Judenschaft 1800–1870." *Jewish Studies in Memory of G. A. Kohut* (1935), pp. 221–225.

44. Through the efforts of R. Moses Teitelbaum (cf., Loew, *Gesammelte Schriften*, II, pp. 76–103). The spread of *Hassidism* was also connected with the emigration of

Jews to Carpatho-Russia and to other regions of Hungary.

45. Of whom the best known were the Darmstatters, the Dérenbourgs, and Solomon Munk.

46. Cf., Grünwald, *Samuel Oppenheimer und sein Kreis*, pp. 68–82.

47. Cf., Weinryb, *Neueste Wirtschaftsgeschichte der Juden in Russland und Polen* (1931), pp. 81–92.

48. The vast crowds that attended Lasker's funeral, and also the special resolution of the American Congress—expressing "sympathy" with the German nation on the passing of the "model citizen" who "by his steadfast and courageous defence of liberal policies strove to ensure the social and political progress of his people"—were no doubt expressions of support for the waning spirit of liberalism in Germany. Bismarck, it will be remembered, returned the resolution to the American envoy with the explicit announcement that he refused to bring it to the notice of the German Reichstag since "his views on the political activities of the deputy Lasker and their consequences were diametrically opposed to those of the American Congress." The burial of Lasker was also a case for demonstration of the liberal forces in Germany. Nevertheless, it will be clear from a study of the contemporary world, German, and Jewish press that the core of the "public mourning for Lasker" was the heartfelt spontaneous Jewish reaction (in part that of those of the German Jewish emigrants to the U.S.A. who had participated in the 1848 revolution).

49. The character of this unique "spiritual communication," which played such an important part in the development of "the Science of Judaism" over a period of roughly forty years (1820–1860), emerges clearly from the correspondence of the leading scholars of the movement (the letters of S. D. Luzzatto, S. Y. Rappoport, Y. S.

Reggio, Jost, Zunz, Geiger, Frankel, Senior Sacks, and many others). The whole subject merits a special sociohistorical study.

50. This is, in fact, the actual historical content of the polemical debate about the autonomy of the community in purely Jewish affairs and its power of excommunication. Mendelssohn on principle opposed giving the community this power and his stand was typical of the whole *Haskalah* movement.

51. Cf. Julius Guttmann, *Philosophies of Judaism* (Philadelphia, 1964), pp. 289–290.

52. This was also the reason why Mommsen, in his pamphlet *Auch ein Wort über unser Judentum*, Berlin, 1880, pp. 15–16, issued a warning—from his own standpoint—that the proliferation of "Jewish associations" was a hindrance to the process of assimilation, since these associations did not merely help to keep the "corporate body of Jewry" in existence, but actually strengthened it.

53. Revolutionary methods of political influence had already, as is well known, been employed to bring about the Emancipation at the time of the French Revolution: deputations of Jews to the National Assembly, petitions by ordinary citizens, the intervention of the Paris municipality, etc. The inclusion of equal rights for the Jews in the platform of the liberal parties in the nineteenth century was also a direct result of Jewish membership in those parties. In all the countries of Europe, the methods employed by the Jews, generally speaking, were those of public defense, protest meetings, parliamentary questions, etc.

54. International cooperation in anti-Semitism takes—and took—various forms. It is to be regretted that this aspect of the phenomenon of anti-Semitism has not been given sufficiently close scientific study. This applies not only

to the literary material, but also to the important documentary evidence. This is quite apart, of course, from the fact that the persecution of Jews in one country strengthens the forces of anti-Semitism in all the others. A particularly instructive illustration of this is the reciprocal influence of German and Russian anti-Semitism.

55. Cf. Wiener, *Jüdische Religion im Zeitalter der Emanzipation* (Berlin 1933), p. 174. Also Geiger's editorial article in *Wissenschaftliche Zeitschrift,* Vol. I (1835).

56. Cf. Ahad Ha-am, *Al Perashat Derakhim,* Pt. III, *Yalqut Qatan* 19 and 33. Also Geiger's interesting letter to Bischoffsheim (*Nachgelassene Schriften,* V, p. 348) in which he too speaks of "the people's inner feeling" and its function in the history of the Jewish religion and the reforms made in it.

57. Cf. *The Life of Solomon Maimon,* Pt. II, Chap. 12.

58. Holdheim, *Über die Autonomie der Rabbiner und das Prinzip der jüdischen Ehe* (1843), pp. 60, 88–89, 96, 134–136, 143–150. Also Mendelssohn, *Jerusalem.*

59. Cf. Holdheim, *op. cit.*

60. Cf. *Protokolle und Aktenstücke der zweiten Rabbiner— Versammlung zu Frankfurt am Main* (1845), pp. 18–19.

61. Such an appeal to the authorities was usually a sign not only of the acuteness of the crisis, but also of its functional character, that is, of the feeling in the community that the "Jewish authorities" were not performing their appointed task.

62. This was the *halakhic* justification of those rabbis who encouraged Jewish participation in the uprising in Poland (R. Bear Meizlish), or supported the plans of the Russian revolutionaries for the confiscation of the great landowners' estate (R. Izhak Rabinowitz of Ponevyezh).

63. In this connection, cf., the first steps taken by the Jewish socialists in defense of their people against anti-Semitic attacks, *Historische Schriften*, Vol. III, pp. 787–791. A similar stand had already been adopted by certain Jewish circles at the time of the French Revolution.

64. Cf. Riesser's letter in which he discusses his plans for leaving Germany and stresses his weariness with the whole struggle for civic equality: Gabriel Riesser's *Gesammelte Schriften*, p. 219 (his letter to Dr. Steinheim of September 20, 1836); cf. also, *ibid.*, pp. 236–237. And see the article by M. Braun, "Aus H. Graetzens Lern- und Wanderjahren," *MGWJ* (1910), p. 351.

65. Cf. Moses Hess, *Rome and Jerusalem*, letter 13; particularly the emphasis on the fact that a "native land" is a prerequisite for any organization of the nation's life on the basis of manual labor and, in general, for any progressive form of social order.

66. One of the fundamental features of the program drawn up by Rabbi Akivah Yosef Schlesinger (the founder of the *Hamaaleh* association) was the desire to establish a powerful Jewish authority that should be able to punish transgressors and rigorously enforce the observance of the Torah and *mitzvot*.

67. On the decline of the congregations in the time of the movements for Enlightenment and Emancipation cf., Baron, *The Jewish Community*, II, pp. 351–366.

68. The truth of this assumption is borne out by a general survey of the large number of different associations, societies, chapters and federations, and of their connection with the movements and trends of the period preceding the rise of Zionism (*Haskalah*, religious reform, the struggle for emancipation, defense against anti-Semitism, mutual aid, etc.).

69. Cf., e.g., the remarks of Moritz Lazarus in his article "Was heisst National," published in the collected edition of his articles, *Treu und Frei* (1887), p. 76.